When Children Write

Critical Re-Visions of the Writing Workshop

Timothy J. Lensmire

TEACHERS
COLLEGE
PRESS

Teachers College, Columbia University
New York and London

Published by Teachers College Press, 1234 Amsterdam Avenue, New York, N.Y. 10027

Library of Congress Cataloging-in-Publication Data

Lensmire, Timothy J., 1961–
  When children write : critical re-vision of the writing workshop \
Timothy J. Lensmire.
    p.   cm. — (Language and literacy series)
  Includes bibliographical references and index.
  ISBN 0-8077-3329-6 (cloth). — ISBN 0-8077-3328-8 (pbk.)
    1. English language—Composition and exercises—Study and teaching
(Elementary) 2. Group work in education. 3. Interpersonal
relations. I. Title. II. Series: Language and literacy series
(New York, N.Y.) LB1576.L44 1994
  372.6'23—dc20   93-44983

ISBN 0-8077-3328-8 (pbk.)
ISBN 0-8077-3329-6 (cloth)

Printed on acid-free paper
Manufactured in the United States of America
01 00 99 98 97 96 95 94   8 7 6 5 4 3 2 1

Contents

Foreword

In her latest book of essays, Adrienne Rich says she writes best "in solitude in dialogue with community." Writing workshop classrooms around the country are trying to create just that environment for all students, as children hear or read each other's compositions and respond as critics to their author peers. Writing workshops may even be considered one of the best examples of "cooperative learning," so widely advocated for today's schools.

But, like so many excellent ideas, writing workshops are easier to read about than to enact. One potential problem is that relationships among children now affect not just classroom management and classroom climate but the official curriculum—not just in the talk but in the texts. Whose compositions are appreciated by peers and whose are not? Who enjoys praise and constructive advice and who only feels misunderstood? And, perhaps most difficult of all, what should the teacher do when some children turn their peers into story characters, and then portray those characters in hurtful ways?

Timothy Lensmire is not the first researcher to dare to discuss such problems. Anne Dyson's new book in this same series on the experiences of first-grade writers in a racially heterogeneous classroom comes immediately to mind. Her vivid narrative and analysis is written by an outside researcher who focuses most intently on the children. What, we wonder, is—or should be—a teacher's response?

Lensmire is a teacher, and this is his case study of teacher research that led him to rethink his practice of writing workshop with third-grade children. His choice of the term *re-vision* for that rethinking, instead of the more usual *revision,* is just right. It does more than catch the reader's attention with a hyphen. The distinction between *revision* and *re-vision* is the same as Gregory Bateson's distinction between "feedback" and "recalibration" as different ways to perfect adaptive action.

Bateson's most familiar example contrasts two kinds of control of a home heating system by means of a thermostat: one (using feedback) turns the furnace off and on, moment to moment, in response to information about deviation from a preset standard; the other (recalibration) resets the standard when the resident is dissatisfied with the resulting temperature over some period of time.

Several years ago, two colleagues—Judith Diamond and Paul Naso—and I reviewed teacher research on writing these terms. We assumed that in a best case scenario a writing teacher uses both these learning modes. She gets immediate feedback that influences how she conducts her class and also recalibrates the patterning of past learnings each time she acts in class. That's the ideal.

In the more likely reality, the teacher gets feedback on the success of a particular strategy, but not on her body of knowledge about teaching and learning that calibrates those strategies. For any teacher, just getting feedback about how to preserve a steady state in the ever-changing classroom life is infinitely more complex than the dichotomous on/off of the thermostat. And more fundamental change in teaching strategies, recalibration in Bateson's terms, is more complex than in any of his examples.

Lensmire's account shows how teacher research can be an important aid in this process. He set out to create for his students a writing workshop in which a "community" of writers would share their writing and respond to and nurture each other. But what is the teacher to do when one member's "self-expression" hurts another member of that community? When, in John Willinsky's words, "the self finally expressed in student writing is not the one we were hoping to see emerge?"

We follow teacher–researcher Lensmire as he both acts in, and reflects on, the writing workshop in his classroom: planning, arranging, speaking and listening, agonizing, revising, and finally re-visioning—trying new ways to create, within his classroom, that elusive "community." Whatever the subject we teach, there may be no more important objective for today's broken world.

Courtney B. Cazden

REFERENCES

Bateson, G. (1979). *Mind and nature: A necessary unity.* New York: E. P. Dutton.

Cazden, C. B., Diamondstone, J., & Naso, P. (1989). Teachers and researchers: Roles and relationships. *The Quarterly of the National Writing Project and the Center for the Study of Writing, 11*(4), 1–3, 25–27.

Dyson, A. (1993). *Social worlds of children learning to write in an urban primary school.* New York: Routledge.

Rich, A. (1993). *What is found there: Notebooks on poetry and politics.* New York: W.W. Norton.

Willinsky, J. (1990). *The new literacy: Redefining reading and writing in the schools.* New York: Routledge.

Acknowledgments

I relied on the intellectual and emotional supportt of a number of people as I researched and wrote this book. Thank you to David Cohen, Susan Florio-Ruane, David Labaree, Jeremy Price, Arthur Wirth, Diane Beals, Louis Smith, Deborah Ball, Mary Ann Dzuback, Laureen Sosniak, Suzanne Wilson, Lisa Satanovsky, and James Garrison. My thanks also to my editors—Sarah Biondello, Carol Collins, and Leslie Christie—who have been generous with their skill and encouragement.

Finally, thank you to Jane Ritger-Lensmire, and our children, John and Sarah. My hopes for something better in our schools and our society are grounded, ultimately, in the growth and joy that I experience every day of my life with them.

*

A grant from the Spencer Foundation Small Grant Program and a Faculty Research Grant from Washington University supported the completion of this project. Parts of this book first appeared in *Curriculum Inquiry 23* (1993).

Introduction

I thought my story would be a different one. I would teach writing for a year in a third grade public school classroom, struggling a little at first to get a writing workshop running with children who had only exercised their pens filling in worksheet blanks. I would research my own teaching and students' learning. But the workshop would run, and I would focus my attention on what I took to be its heart: talking with individual children in relatively isolated, intimate conversations about their writing—what they were trying to do, what help they needed. Occasionally, I would have to engage children's texts in a sort of ideological critique, pointing to traces of classism, sexism, racism, fighting society's impress on their meanings and values. In the freedom of the workshop, children would choose their topics and purposes for writing, develop their ways of working texts, and write. They would go to each other, they would come to me, for help. My third grade students would write themselves on the page, move, be heard, in a place that habitually constrained their voices and bodies to teacher questions, to desks. Our workshop would be a little Emersonian democracy; Dewey's embryonic community.

I did teach writing for a year, and the children and I did struggle to find a way to go about our work. I talked with children about their texts, and important, fascinating, funny, worthy-of-telling things happened. The children flexed their muscles, wrote, were heard. All of this happened, and I could have told this gratifying story of workshop life without lying—but I would have been lying. Lying because children are not *only* the Romantic, innocent little beings that appear in the stories of workshop advocates. Lying, because neither workshop approaches, nor the role they envision for teachers, are so innocent.

Writing workshop approaches to the teaching of writing emphasize increased control by students over their own writing activities and texts. As I shifted control over aspects of the work of literacy to children in this third grade classroom, children's relations with each other became extremely important for their experiences and writing in the workshop. These relations included the rejection, by children, of members of the other sex as partners in collaborative work, and peer hierarchies granting those girls and boys at the top status and influence, and those at the bottom the brunt of teasing and exclusion. This "hidden curriculum" of the peer culture—a hidden curriculum that I had experienced as a child on the playground and on the bus to school (and had forgotten); that I had experienced as a junior high teacher around the edges of my English class, when I turned from the blackboard in time to see the love letter passed, or saw the tears in Darrel's eyes after another round of whispered abuse from a classmate (and had forgotten)—this hidden curriculum of the peer culture asserted itself in important ways within the official work of our third grade writing workshop. And, I suppose, it was supposed to. Workshop approaches invite the lives of children into the classroom. Children's lives include their relations with each other, in and out of school.

My story focuses on this underside of our workshop community. I examine how a peer culture with gender divisions and informal hierarchies of status and power shaped the production and sharing of texts in our writing workshop. Stated more directly, I worry about how children evaluated each other and divided themselves up along social class and gender lines, despite my interventions as a teacher in this classroom. I explore how certain children silenced other children, in a classroom situation explicitly created to assure that all children's voices would sound and be heard.

In some sense, my story works for a recovery of memory, by asking (and helping) us to remember what it was like to be a child, have friends and enemies, play, tease, and be teased. We are often invited to remember our childhoods in the stories of books and movies. But my story also asks us to look to the future, especially to our futures in classrooms, and ask: What do our experiences and those of the children in my classroom *mean* for how we teach and learn?

These problems have not been taken up in any serious way by writing workshop advocates and other progressive educators and researchers who call for the increased liberation of student intention and association in classrooms—most likely because such writers have pointed, often with good reason, to the traditional teacher and textbook as the primary enemies of student voice in schools. Writing workshop advocates such as Donald Graves (1983), Lucy Calkins (1986), and Donald Murray (1968), tend to tell success stories. Writers such as Anne Dyson (1989) and Vivian Paley (1989, 1990) tell much more complex stories, and do point to peer relations as sources of conflict and toil. But even these stories have a Candide-like quality in which everything, in the end, is for the best. Everything, in the end, is not for the best.

Typically, children compose very little in schools. The writing that is done is tightly controlled by the teacher who initiates writing tasks; determines audience, purpose, and format for the writing; and acts as the sole audience and evaluator. There is little opportunity for revision, and the purpose of such school writing is often to display academic mastery in evaluative contexts. In such situations, students' technical competence to write, and their motivation to use writing in ways that enrich and transform their lives, suffer (Applebee, 1981; Doyle, 1986; Florio-Ruane & Dunn, 1985). Traditional writing instruction functions, then, much like other traditional forms of pedagogy to silence students, deny student experiences and meanings, and alienate students from the teaching and learning they encounter in schools (Everhart, 1983; Freire, 1970, 1985; Waller, 1932).

In contrast, writing workshop approaches emphasize providing opportunities for students to engage in and practice the craft of writing. A central theme within such approaches is student ownership: Students have wide powers to determine the topics, audiences, purposes, and forms of their texts. Such control is in the service of student voice. With the support of the teacher and numerous opportunities to collaborate and share texts with peers, children are supposed to gradually become more and more able to realize their intentions in text. This is the primary goal of such approaches.

Workshop approaches are part of a more general and varied push to teach writing "as a process" (Hairston, 1982). Process writing approaches conceive of writing as a complex cognitive and communicative act, framed by a purpose, and made up of various recursive phases or stages, such as drafting, revision, editing, and publishing (Applebee, 1986). Within such approaches, teachers focus on helping children work through the writing process. Willinsky (1990) provides an even broader home for writing workshop and process approaches within "The New Literacy," his name for approaches to the teaching of reading, writing, and literature, that share a commitment to increased control by students over meaning and texts in the classroom, with consequent changes in the roles and activities of teachers and students there.

I remain sympathetic to, and see my work as contributing to, "New Literacy" efforts. It is essential to put meaning-making at the center of literacy work with children, to enliven and transform classrooms with the voices and texts of children. But we need to critically appropriate the assumptions and practices of workshop approaches, something I had barely begun to do as I started my teaching and research at Clifford Elementary School in the fall of 1989. Looking back, I would say of myself and my assumptions something like William Morris said of a fellow 19th century socialist, Sidney Webb, who thought evolutionary processes assured the coming of socialism:

> He is so anxious to prove the commonplace that our present industrial system embraces some of the machinery by means of which a socialist system might be worked . . . that his paper tends to produce the impression of one who thinks that we are already in the first stage of socialist life. . . . [Webb overestimates] the importance of the *mechanism* of a system of society apart from the *end* towards which it may be used. (cited in Williams, 1983, p. 183)

I put too much faith in a workshop "system," in its processes and routines, and had not worried enough about its content and ends. Or, perhaps more correctly, it was not until I had lived and worked in a writing workshop with young children for an extended period of time that I realized there was reason for worry. The third graders in my class— James, Maya, Jil, Karen, John, Jessie, and the rest[1]—taught me much about workshop approaches, much about themselves and writing in classrooms, about teaching and its responsibilities.

———

As a teacher-researcher in this writing workshop, I wanted to study what the commitment to increased student control over the work of literacy entailed for my teaching and my students' learning and experiences. I brought interpretive research assumptions and methods (Bogdan & Biklen, 1982; Erickson, 1986; Hammersly & Atkinson, 1983) to this work, and collected the following types of data:

1. Fieldnotes. I wrote fieldnotes following each day of teaching. These notes included general narratives of the day's teaching, as well as reflections on specific pedagogical and methodological problems and issues.
2. Teacher and classroom documents. I collected lesson plans, lists of rules and procedures, forms, sign-in book used in writing workshop library, notes to students and parents, etc. These documents provided written records of teacher and student intentionality (Burton, 1985), and enabled me to reexamine what we had hoped would happen, in order to juxtapose these hopes against what actually occurred in the classroom.
3. Audiotapes. Starting in October, I taped whole-class sessions and writing conferences with children in order to do close analyses of discourse in various workshop situations.

4. Student interviews. Twenty-four of twenty-seven children in the class participated in interviews conducted at the end of the school year by colleagues of mine. The extended interviews focused on the sense students were making of the writing workshop, and included questions that explored children's relations with one another and with their teachers, and how these relations influenced their writing.
5. Student writing. Students' written work—both rough drafts and finished pieces—was photocopied throughout the year. These texts were essential for analyzing the material and genres children pursued in their writing, and how children's texts were related to the immediate social context.

In this book, I pursue three interrelated subjects, and work productively at the boundaries of more traditional research in elementary classrooms.

The first subject is my experiences as a teacher in this writing workshop—a teacher committed to helping children "come to voice," both in the sense of the expression of a unique self, and the sense of greater public participation in the cultural work of naming and renaming the world and their places in it (Hooks, 1989). I write from the point of view of a teacher-researcher of writing who hopes not only to understand what is happening, but also to act effectively and responsibly in response (Bissex & Bullock, 1987; Goswami & Stillman, 1987). In such work, the classroom becomes a "philosophical laboratory," a site for the application and revision of theory through practice (Berthoff, 1987).

The second subject of my book is the examination of writing workshop approaches as an agenda for writing classrooms, and as a strategy for the creation of more humane and just forms of life in school and society. Writing workshop assumptions, goals and practices are scrutinized and revised. To accomplish this, I confront workshop approaches with the concerns and insights of the language and literary theories of Bakhtin (1981, 1986), and the critical pedagogy and theory perspectives of Freire (1970, 1985) and Habermas (1984, 1987), among others. I bring literary and philosophical perspectives to my analyses that have informed some work on composition pedagogy and theory at the college level (eg., Berlin, 1988; Faigley, 1986; Harris, 1987), but that have seldom been used to illuminate work with elementary students.

My students' experiences in this writing workshop is the final and dominant subject of my book. Children's intentions for writing, their relations with peers and teachers, their struggles, their texts, are at the heart of this work. Erickson and Shultz (1992) have noted that

> Virtually no research has been done that places student experience
> at the center of attention. We do not see student interests and their
> known and unknown fears. . . . Classroom research typically does
> not ask what the student is up to. (pp. 467, 468)

What my third grade students were "up to" in this writing workshop is
the primary theme of my book, and drives my exploration and criticism
of writing workshop goals and practices.

In my first chapter, "Beginnings," I articulate the goals for teaching writing that I brought to my work with these third graders, and elaborate my
initial conception of the teacher's role in writing workshops. I begin to
examine what happened to these hopes and intentions in my second
chapter, "Teacher-Researcher Practice." The chapter traces three progressions in my work and thought as a teacher-researcher: a move from
being *the* writing teacher to *a* writing teacher in the room; the evolution
of my research methods in the face of conflicting teacher and researcher
demands; and a shifting research focus, from primary concern with my
own experiences as a teacher to an emphasis on student experiences and
writing within the social context of the workshop.

I take up the experiences and texts of my third grade students in the
core chapters of my book. Chapter 3, "Student Intention and Relations,"
focuses on the texts and activities of a popular and powerful group of
boys in the classroom, led by James. I argue that James and his friends
asserted their dominant position among peers not only in their face-to-
face interactions with others, but also in subtle ways in their texts. I show
how these young writers resisted teacher interventions into their writing,
and drew on gender arrangements and common forms of teasing
between boys and girls to provoke response from peers.

In chapter 4, "Peer Audiences and Risk," and chapter 5, "Fiction, Distance and Control," I concentrate on children with little status and influence among peers, and use discussions of their experiences to characterize common student responses to this workshop as a context for
writing and sharing texts. I draw heavily on children's interviews, as well
as children's texts and classroom vignettes, in order to specify:

- the risks that children, especially unpopular children, associated
  with writing for peer audiences;
- children's responses to those risks, which included rejecting certain peers as audiences, and avoiding genres and topics that
  involved too much exposure of self; and

- the reasons children in this workshop preferred fictional narratives to the personal narratives I encouraged them to write, which included their belief that fiction involved less responsibility for what was written, and a sense of control and pleasure in the writing of fiction that they did not feel when writing about what "really happened."

Children's texts participated, for better and for worse, in the social lives of children in the workshop. My sixth chapter, "Teacher Response to Children's Texts," tells the story of my response to Maya's text, *The Zit Fit: The Lovers in the School.* Maya, a popular child in the class, wanted to publish a fictional narrative that I read as an attack on an unpopular classmate. I explore how my response was caught up in the social relations, norms, and public sharing of texts in the writing workshop, as well as larger debates on the status of texts in the world and writers' responsibilities for what they write.

Across these core chapters, I challenge workshop advocates' Romantic portrayals of children and writing—portrayals that tend to abstract young writers and their texts from social context, and place the meanings and values of their texts beyond criticism. In my final chapter, "Workshop Re-Visions," I link a revised conception of children as writers to two proposals for change in the work of teachers in writing workshops. The first is a revised conception of teacher response to children's text; the second, an increased role for teachers as curriculum-makers in writing classrooms.

The overall goal of these revisions, as well as the close examination of children's experiences and writing in this writing workshop, is to articulate and address problems and issues that teachers face when they teach in ways that respect student agency and voice, but that have not been adequately treated in the how-to books of workshop advocates, in research on teaching and learning writing, and in discussions of progressive and radical approaches to education. In what follows, I bring some of these problems to our larger collective conversation on teaching and learning in schools.

NOTE

[1] These and all other student and school personnel names are pseudonyms, as is the name of the school; see Appendix for discussion of my use of pseudonyms.

Chapter 1

Beginnings

My history as a writer might best be traced to writing conferences (actually, usually, arguments) I had with my mother at the kitchen table. I remember writing a paper on William Faulkner's *As I Lay Dying* (Darl Bundren was my hero) for a high school literature class, and a short, short, story about mutant life forms growing under my bed when I was a seventh grader at St. Mary's Catholic school. I would take them to my mother and always get more help than I wanted. She would read my texts, point to a place on the page, and say, "What does this mean?" I would grudgingly explain, and then defend the adequacy of my written words against any changes.

I am certain that these arguments, focused on meaning rather than punctuation or spelling, were a healthy training ground for becoming a teacher of writing. But I *became* a teacher of writing when I read Donald Murray's *A Writer Teaches Writing: A Practical Method of Teaching Composition* (1968) the summer before my 2nd year as a seventh grade English teacher in Northern Wisconsin.

I had been teaching seventh grade English with little formal preparation for it. I had started as a music major in college, and then switched to elementary education. Before the English position, I worked with sixth graders in an elementary school, and taught eighth grade Math, Civics, and English in a junior high. I brought a love of literature (especially American literature) to my teaching, but again with little formal training—I took my lessons from Twain and Steinbeck in the park during summer, and late at night, in bed.

I was supposed to teach writing to my seventh graders, but was in the dark about how to go about it. I got Murray's book from a colleague, studied it, and from that point on thought of myself as a writing teacher who also happened to have other required duties—some I deemed worthy and others not so—in his English classes. Worthy ones were sharing a novel or two, short stories, plays and poetry with my seventh graders; not so were weekly spelling lists and grammar usage exercises in preparation for district tests.

Murray seduced me. His descriptions of engaged students writing of what they cared about, and teachers helping and coaching them, spoke directly to disappointments and hopes I had collected in my early teaching experiences. Later, when I read Murray's (1979) "The Listening Eye: Reflections on the Writing Conference," the teaching of writing seemed to return to the kitchen table: Murray waits in his office, winter and dark outside, for Andrea and her rough draft and "this strange, exposed kind of teaching, one on one."

Willinsky (1990) correctly claims that the primary appeal of workshop approaches like Murray's is not so much any new teaching techniques and materials, but more a vision of teaching and learning with students. The appeal is in the transformation of teacher and student roles, in relations that grant students a more active place in their learning and teachers the chance to stand beside and help students, rather than lord it over them. My turn to writing workshop approaches was a Romantic response to alienating student and teacher work—I wanted students to be alive rather than deadened by mechanical, boring school tasks. Murray's approach asked students to look to their own experiences and imagination for material. It offered a new way to work literacy in the classroom.

So that year I began to teach writing in ways that approximated workshop approaches. My primary moves were to grant students increased control over the topics and purposes of what they wrote, and to increase their access to each other as collaborators and audiences. And most responded. They wrote. They listened respectfully to classmates' pieces, laughed with me at intended and unintended humor. I got tired rip-offs of Star Trek, and dutiful (this still was school, after all) reflections on "my favorite pet." But I also got Jenny's "Lyon, Lyon," a parody of Blake's "The Tyger." I was using Kenneth Koch's (1973) *Rose, where did you get that red?*, and had some of my classes write poems and stories in response to Blake's poem. Jenny appropriated Blake's unusual spelling, his use of questions to describe the cat and wonder at creation, and the repetition of the first stanza at the end of the poem; she degraded most everything else. Instead of Blake's tyger, and its "fearful symmetry" and "deadly terrors," Jenny's peers and I encountered a beer-guzzling lyon, overweight, flatulent, unfit to be king of the jungle. At times, I persuaded myself that my classroom bustled with properly irreverent Romantic poets.

I would take their work to other teachers. A few would smile approvingly, and share their students' texts with me. Most would look at me with puzzled faces. Their glances, and sometimes their words, would ask, "So? Why are you doing this?" I was often confused (and hurt) by their responses. I had already accomplished the primary goal I had for my writing classes: simply to get children who usually resisted writing to pick up a pencil and write, and share their work with others. The teacherly satisfaction I felt did not inhere so much in the quality of the texts or what was said, but in the fact that they had been written at all.

But my colleagues' glances and questions haunted me, forced me to admit that I could neither articulate why I was doing what I was doing, nor argue its importance. Their questions haunted me in the classroom sometimes, when I faced a student who wanted help, and I didn't know what to say, at least partly because I didn't know what I wanted the student to do, other than write.

When I left teaching to go to graduate school, I took my interest in progressive approaches to teaching writing with me, and made the cultural, political, and social aspects of language and literacy the focus of my work. As I studied, I began to find answers to the earlier questions of purpose and worth with which my teaching colleagues had confronted me. My reading, research and writing helped me develop a broad conception of literacy—a critical literacy—that emphasized its contribution to student empowerment and participation, in schools and a society that denied participation to so many by gender, race and class (Freire & Macedo, 1987; Giroux, 1988; McLeod, 1986).

My work at Clifford Elementary School took me back to the public school classroom, back to teaching writing. In what follows, I elaborate the two goals that I brought to this project for teaching writing within writing workshops. These goals are developed around the concept of voice. Actually, two related senses of voice: one artistic and aimed at naming yourself; the other political and focused on naming the world.

———

Children want to write. They want to write the first day they attend school. This is no accident. Before they went to school they marked up walls, pavements, newspapers with crayons, chalk, pens or pencils . . . anything that makes a mark. The child's marks say, "I am."

"No, you aren't," say most school approaches to the teaching of writing. (Graves, 1983, p. 3)

My first broad goal focused on the individual's expression of *subjectivity*, leading, on the one side, to the production of a verbal object of art, and on the other, to self-understanding and self-creation. It emphasized the private work of finding your own voice in your writing, a voice that says, as Graves puts it, "I am." Writing, here, is the expression of something inside with the help of external signs. Finding your voice involves looking to your own experiences for what it is you want to say. Writing is conceived of as the process (sometimes the struggle) of expressing and organizing personal experience:

> By articulating experience, we reclaim it for ourselves. Writing allows us to turn the chaos into something beautiful, to frame selected moments in our lives, to uncover and to celebrate the organizing patterns of our existence. (Calkins, 1986, p. 3)

There are strong affinities here to Emerson, Thoreau, American Romanticism—a celebration of experience and an individualistic, non-conformist strain—evident in Calkins' call to make something beautiful out of "moments in our lives," and Graves' affirmation of the child's "I am" against the erasing institutional forces of schooling. Like Thoreau (1960), workshop approaches would have young writers

> Drive life into a corner, reduce it to its lowest terms, and, if it proved mean, why then to get the whole and genuine meanness of it, and publish its meanness to the world; or if it were sublime, to know it by experience, and be able to give a true account of it. (p. 66)

Graves and Calkins seldom seem to consider that life might be mean at its "lowest terms," but Thoreau's rhetoric is appropriate for workshop approaches. The image is one of burrowing deep into subjectivity, past "the mud and slush of opinion, and prejudice, and tradition" to discover your authentic nature, and a voice that expresses who you are. When you do, the words on the page are your words, not someone else's.

But *your* words, of course, are always someone else's words first, and these words sound with the intonations and evaluations of others who have used them before, and from whom you learned them. As Bakhtin (1981) reminds us, the romantic poet "is not, after all, the first speaker, the one who disturbs the eternal silence of the universe" (p. 69)—the poet learned her words from others, indeed, became a self she could point to and ask questions of in this sharing of words and gestures.

The shift here is from what Berlin (1988) calls an "expressionistic" rhetoric, characterized by Romantic and idealistic conceptions of mind and language, to a "social-epistemic" one, in which language mediates a dynamic interrelation of individuals with material and social aspects of their environment. My introduction to this rhetoric was provided by Vygotsky (1978, 1979, 1981). Within Vygotsky's social-psychological framework, consciousness arises out of social interaction. Speech is fundamental to thought for Vygotsky, with higher mental functions developing in its context, and with the structures and processes of thought conceptualized in relation to the structures and processes of speech. Internalized (inner) speech is, for Vygotsky, the very fabric and process of thought itself.

But I soon grew frustrated with the seeming neutrality and emotional flatness of social interaction in the hands of Vygotsky and some of his interpreters (e.g., Wertsch, 1979, 1985). Where were heated arguments at the kitchen table and in the classroom, ideological conflict, power, passion? Social interaction was smoothed out, and so was much of the complexity and emotional toil of inner speech, of thought, of writing.

I turned to the work of Bakhtin and his circle of friends and colleagues. Like Vygotsky, Bakhtin and his circle asserted a social account of mind in which consciousness emerges in our relations with each other (see Volosinov, 1973, 1976). But unlike Vygotsky, this process, and consciousness itself, is charged with emotion and struggle over meaning and values. The Bakhtin circle presents "language use itself as a locus of class and group conflict" (LaCapra, 1983, p. 320). Our days and our consciousnesses are filled with living language, with the words of others.

> The word in language is half someone else's. It becomes "one's own" only when the speaker populates it with his own intention, his own accent, when he appropriates the word, adapting it for his own semantic and expressive intention. . . . And not all words for just anyone submit easily to this appropriation, to this seizure and transformation into private property: many words stubbornly resist, others remain alien, sound foreign in the mouth of the one who appropriated them and who now speaks them . . . it is as if they put themselves in quotation marks against the will of the speaker. . . . Expropriating [language], forcing it to submit to one's own intentions and accents, is a difficult and complicated process. (Bakhtin, 1981, p. 294)

As Bakhtin became more and more important for my conceptions of language and writing, I did not lose the goal for my students of helping them find individual voices—the goal just looked a little different. When consciousness is viewed as developing through social interaction—when thought is "inner speech" that emerges as the child engages others in investigations of the world—then finding your own voice is *less* burrowing to some authentic nature, and *more* appropriating the myriad voices and words surrounding you, and forcing them to your own purposes. I assumed, like Graves, that children wanted to say, "I am." My students would write texts that expressed this uniqueness. I assumed with Rorty (1989) that

> The conscious need of the strong poet to *demonstrate* that he is not a copy or replica [is] merely a special form of an unconscious need everyone has; the need to come to terms with the blind impress which chance has given him, to make a self for himself by redescribing that impress in terms which are, if only marginally, his own. (p. 43)

My classroom would be a place for children to begin to rework the blind impress, a place to look to their experiences, and in remembering them and reworking them in their writing, to name themselves rather than be named by others. My first goal for workshop writing, then, emphasized a private project in which young writers were increasingly able to find their voices—to find what they had to say and wanted to say—in their texts.

I also brought a second, political sense of voice to my work at Clifford Elementary School. This sense of voice emphasizes an individual's or group's active participation in the world, an active part in the production of knowledge and texts. If the first sense of voice is evoked with the contrast, "my words versus another's words," then the contrast to this political sense of voice is *silence*, where silence points to oppressive conditions that keep certain people from participating in decision making, storytelling. Voice here, stands for active engagement by a given speaker or writer in the community and society. Rather than emphasize the individual's attempts to *distinguish* herself from others with her texts, this sense of voice emphasizes a writer inserting herself and her texts into public spheres.

Freire's (1970, 1985) work was most influential for my sense of this political connotation of voice. His critique of traditional schooling practices emphasizes the passivity of students in traditional pedagogies, the reduction of learners to objects, when they should be subjects of their learning. He names this sort of education the "banking conception of education."

> The scope of action allowed to students extends only as far as receiving, filing, and storing the deposits. . . . In the last analysis, it is people themselves who are filed away through the lack of creativity, transformation, and knowledge in this (at best) misguided system. For apart from inquiry, apart from the praxis, people cannot be truly human. Knowledge emerges only through invention and reinvention, through restless, impatient, continuing, hopeful inquiry people pursue in the world, with the world, and with each other. (1970, p. 58)

Freire's pedagogy, what he calls "cultural action for freedom" in his *The Politics of Education* (1985), emphasizes engaging students in dialogues focused on their existential situation, an ongoing inquiry into their world in which they formulate increasingly critical interpretations of that world and their place in it. From this perspective, the power to name the world and order it has rested, in society, with the elite, and in the classroom, with the teacher and textbooks. Freire's pedagogy seeks to upset this power relation with *student voices*, and help students actively participate in making sense of the world around them. Hooks (1989) captures this sense of voice as an act of individual and collective resistance to domination by others in her discussion of the importance of "coming to voice" in feminist work.

> For women within oppressed groups who have contained so many feelings—despair, rage, anguish—who do not speak, as poet Audre Lorde writes, "for fear our words will not be heard nor welcomed," coming to voice is an act of resistance. Speaking becomes both a way to engage in active self-transformation and a rite of passage where one moves from being object to being subject. Only as subjects can we speak. As objects we remain voiceless—our beings defined and interpreted by others. (p. 12)

In my classroom, I wanted students to come to voice, in both the sense of a private exploration and ordering of experience in the expression of a unique self, and the sense of greater public participation in the cultural work of naming and renaming the world and their places within it. Both senses of voice suggest resistance—the first resistance to Dewey's "crust of convention," the second to power relations that silence.

I wanted to set up and work in a transformed classroom community. My dreams for that community emphasized the presence of student voices where there used to be primarily the teacher's, and constrained, lifeless student responses to alienating material. I envisioned, with echoes of Emerson, a miniature cultural democracy, a marketplace of ideas and stories, in which strong individuals asserted themselves, and continually provoked and enhanced each other in their interactions (West, 1989). My classroom, like Dostoevsky's novels, would celebrate heteroglossia: unofficial voices, the polyphonic confusion of voices sounding with the characteristic words and intonations of different social groups, and the idiosyncratic twists of speakers and writers attempting to force shared, given words to individual, particular purposes and situations (Pechey, 1986; Bakhtin, 1981).

My role as the teacher was to encourage, orchestrate, and support this heteroglossia, finding ways to help each student sound and be heard. More concretely, I saw myself as pursuing primarily two teacherly tasks. One was creating a classroom environment that supported children's writing. The second was responding to children's texts in writing conferences.

———

I planned to teach each day for approximately 45 minutes. The workshop would follow a three-part routine, with an opening meeting, writing time, and sharing time. The first part of the routine, the opening meeting, would last approximately 5 to 10 minutes, and was modeled after what Calkins (1986) calls mini-lessons. I would use this time to teach, often in a whole-class situation, procedures and norms of the writing workshop, and aspects of the craft of writing.

For example, I would discuss the purposes and handling of the writing folders children and I would use to collect their writing across the year and to monitor their progress. Or we would discuss procedures for working with and maintaining writing tools in the workshop: pens, markers, staplers, paper for rough drafts, scissors for cutting and pasting texts during revision. I would also engage children in activities to help them support and encourage each other as writers in the workshop, particularly in their responses to other children's texts in peer conferences. Workshop approaches encourage teachers and children to think of children as teachers of writing in the classroom. One of the responsibilities of workshop teachers, then, is to ensure that children respect and help each other in their interactions with peers. I would also teach children about how to find topics and brainstorm for ideas, how to draft, revise, edit, and publish pieces in the workshop. I would read books by adult and children authors, and engage them in discussions of what we enjoyed and valued in the books we read, and what we might learn about crafting texts from other authors.

The second part of the routine, lasting approximately 30 minutes, would be called writing time. This was the part of the workshop where children would exercise the greatest control over their own work and movement. This autonomy was to serve their writing, allow them to engage in topics and stories that they found meaningful, and to engage their peers and me in ways and at times that suited their work and the problems they faced as they wrote. If a child needed to talk with someone about an idea she had for the revision of a story, for example, she would have the freedom to do so. She could go to her peers, or, if I was not talking to another child at that moment, to me. Primary activities for children during this time would be brainstorming, drawing, drafting, revising, and editing texts; conferencing with peers and the teacher; publishing selected texts (including putting together books and illustrating stories); and reading. Children would make choices during this time as to what they wanted to work on, with whom, and for how long. My primary activity would be talking with children about their writing. I would help them identify important stories, revise, and get their drafts ready for typing and publishing.

The final 10 minutes or so of the workshop routine would be sharing time (modeled after Graves and Hansen's [1983] "author's chair"). Sharing time would be one of two primary ways for children's texts to go public within the classroom, to reach a larger audience than those in teacher and peer conferences. During sharing time, one or more children would read their texts in front of the class, and then receive response from classmates and adults in the room. The texts would often be finished pieces, typed, illustrated, and bound between cardboard covers. Other times, an author might want response to an earlier draft of a text, perhaps seeking specific help with a writing problem.

The second official way for children to reach the classroom audience would be the workshop library—a few shelves somewhere in the room that housed children's published pieces. Children would donate the books to the library for certain amounts of time so that other children could check them out and read them during writing time and other parts of the school day.

This was my workshop architecture and system. It provided spaces, in writing time, for children to pursue important individual projects, and in sharing time and the workshop library, to make those projects public. The workshop would be alive with student voices in the hum of conferences and collaboration, and the dramatic reading of important texts by child authors. I would support these voices by providing opportunities to write on meaningful topics, by helping children acquire skills of the craft of writing, by shaping a supportive physical and social environment.

My real work, however, and what I looked forward to most in my teaching, was talking with children about their texts. My first conception of response was to follow the child. It drew heavily on Murray, Graves, and Calkins, and their ideas on response. But even before I started teaching at Clifford, I began developing a second conception of teacher response to children's texts that attempted to address problems the first ignored. This second conception recognized that there would be times when children's writing should be questioned, not followed.

The purpose of teacher response within writing workshop approaches is conceived largely in terms of helping students to realize their intentions in text—that is to improve the texts at hand and engage children in conversations that will eventually be internalized and allow them, in the future, to deal more effectively with text on their own. The teacher, once the sole initiator and audience/evaluator of student writing, now *follows the child* (Graves, 1983, p. 103) in his writing processes, watching carefully for ways to encourage, support, model, and coach at appropriate times.

A major concern of workshop advocates is helping teachers avoid falling into traditional, teacher-dominated ways of talking with students and responding to their writing. With reference to Graves, Murray (1985) presents the following basic pattern for writing conferences.

- The student COMMENTS on the draft.
- The teacher READS or reviews the draft.
- The teacher RESPONDS to the student's comments.
- The student RESPONDS to the teacher's response. (p. 148; emphasis in the original)

Graves and Murray want to shake up typical classroom talk in which the teacher leads, the student responds, and the teacher evaluates student response (Cazden, 1986). Instead, they would have the teacher and student engage in a conversation about the craft of writing, a "professional discussion between writers about what works and what needs work" (Murray, 1985, p. 140).

Calkins (1986) brings similar goals and concerns to her writing about teacher response, but tends to emphasize teachers responding to the meaning, the content, of what children are writing. She asserts that teachers must really listen to what children are saying so the children know that they have been heard.

> Our first job in a conference, then, is to be a person, not just a teacher. It is to enjoy, to care, and to respond. We cry, laugh, nod, and sigh. . . . Sometimes that is enough. Sometimes the purpose of a conference is simply to respond. Other times, if the moment seems right, we try, in a conference, to extend what the youngster can do as a writer. (p. 119)

Calkins wants teachers to become a genuine audience for students, an audience that is interested in what young writers have to say. She is responding to the pervasive role of teachers as evaluators of student writing for grading purposes, in which teachers read student texts as tests of students' subject matter knowledge and/or their ability to produce well-spelled words, well-punctuated sentences, and well-organized paragraphs.

With Graves, Murray, and Calkins, I was developing the notion of a teacher response that I call "following the child." This notion suggested beginning assumptions and commitments for the pedagogy and curriculum of the writing instruction I would provide in my work with third grade writers. If we think of pedagogy as a "deliberate attempt to influence how and what knowledge and identities are produced within and among particular sets of social relations" (Giroux & Simon, 1989, p. 239), then following the child, as a pedagogy, seeks to radically upset the micropolitics of social relations and language in the classroom. The commitment to student experience and meaning-making lets students speak *first*, metaphorically (and sometimes literally in writing conferences), in their texts, and in their talk with teachers. Following the child, then, suggests a *how* of writing instruction and teacher response. It also points to the *what*, the curriculum, of writing workshop approaches, and this was where my problems with following the child, as a conception of response, began. Eventually, these problems pushed me to a second conception of response, that is, response as socioanalysis.

The primary curriculum of writing workshop approaches is the purposes, content, and genres, students bring to their writing. Children make curricular decisions, and teachers follow them. Teachers engage children in conversations focused on the craft of writing that assume, that accept, the purposes and content children bring to them. Remember, the primary goal of these conversations is to help children realize their intentions in text, now and in the future.

But what about situations in which student intentions are questionable, such as when a racist joke represents the authentic voice of one of our students?

Willinsky (1986, 1990) frames the problem as one in which the pursuit of art, with an emphasis on self-expression, comes in conflict with the demands of education. He argues that writing workshop approaches have their roots in Romanticism, and that

> The educator drawn to the aesthetic of romanticism must ultimately
> bring together the opposing moments of art and education, providing the opportunity and motive for unfettered expression and then
> the imposition of reflection upon it. (1986, p. 13)

The moral Willinsky draws above emerges from his research with a teacher colleague in a grade one and two classroom. When given the chance to write on topics and in genres of their choosing, the boys in the class wrote violent story after violent story, "until, it seemed, their pens dripped with blood and not an illustration passed without the tell-tale scar of the red marker" (1990, p. 128). The girls wrote of beautiful gardens for mother and daughter to walk in (after doing the dishes), or stories where "princesses wake up, dance with princes all the night long, and the woods laugh out loud" (p. 130). He concludes that to be responsible in our teaching, the progressive commitment to student expression and meaning must be met by an equally progressive commitment to "educate what is traditionally given in gender and identity" (p. 126).

Traditionally given. Willinsky is making two sensible demands here. First, he asks us to recognize that children's stories have *content*, that children's texts represent more than just vehicles for discussions of *process*. Second, he wants us to remember that children work with material from their experiences; or, as Bakhtin might put it, children's material is half someone else's, and appropriated by children for their own purposes. Student experience, what writing workshop advocates want to bring into the classroom, encompasses not only values and knowledge supportive of our goals for learning and moral and political development. Our children grow up in a sexist, racist, classist society. They bring this with them as well.

Writing workshop advocates ignore such issues in their talk about teacher response. Children's stories remain cozily wrapped in a Romantic rhetoric emphasizing personal artistic creativity, "the innocent perceptions of children making individual sense of the world and their role in it" (Gilbert, 1989, p. 199). Graves and Murray focus on crafting texts and avoid the content of student writing, except to say that we should validate it and help students express it more effectively. Calkins emphasizes the content of children's writing more than Graves and Murray in her writing on response, but if you remember the possible responses Calkins lists above—enjoy, care, cry, laugh, nod, sigh—it seems that children will always work with material we should want to support and extend.

My conception of teacher response as following the child was in trouble. It depended on the assumption that children would choose writing tasks that were appropriate for their development as writers and as future citizens of a society with democratic and egalitarian ideals. I needed a conception of teacher response that would retain the commitment to student experience and meaning-making, but that did not place the teacher in an uncritical stance in relation to student intention and content.

———

As part of another project investigating the concept of resistance in various disciplines and practices, I began reading Freud and other writers on psychoanalysis. I was soon struck by similarities in method, material, and social setting, between psychoanalysis and the workshop approaches and conceptions of response I was studying.

As to method, London (1986) notes, in his discussion of "insight therapies" (of which psychoanalysis is the charter member), that

> The patient initiates the talking and assumes responsibility for it. . . . Therapists guide, as it were, by following the patient's lead. . . . All insight therapy therefore involves an insight bearing sequence of 1) exposure by the patient, 2) therapist operation on the exposed material, and 3) consciousness or insight, intellectual or emotional, growing in the patient. (pp. 55, 57)

The pedagogical sequence here is very similar to that in Graves (and Freire)—London even uses similar language when he writes that therapists follow the patient's lead. In the workshop, student experience is elicited, followed by conversations around this material, leading to greater control over writing and self-understanding (in Freire's work, critical consciousness).

For material, psychoanalysis turns to the past, to memory, in order to rework powerful childhood experiences. Writing workshop approaches make a similar turn in their emphasis on children telling personal narratives, and writing on topics they find personally meaningful. Freud asked his patients to free associate to generate this material; Elbow (1973) asked his readers/writers to free write. (See Besley, 1986, for discussion of Romantic origins of Freud's "unconscious"; and Willinsky, 1990, p. 204, for common roots of psychoanalysis and "New Literacy" approaches.)

And in the social setting of psychoanalysis, we return to the isolated pair, alone with their words, and Murray's "strange, exposed kind of teaching." Calkins certainly wants teachers to be warm and supportive in their writing conferences with children, in contrast to the neutral, scientific stance Freud endorsed for analysts in his writing, if not in his own practice (Flax, 1990; Gay, 1988). But the image is powerful—writing conferences and psychoanalysis are enacted by two people, removed from the everyday, focused on the verbal and written texts at hand.

But it was a crucial *difference* between psychoanalysis and "following the child," amid the similarities, that made their juxtaposition especially productive. That difference was the analyst's critical stance in relation to the patient's material. Analysts, unlike workshop teachers, assume that the *content* of their patients' stories demands response and questioning.

I began thinking of response as a type of analysis, but not one supported by Freudian theories of the unconscious, repression, and resistance (even though some researchers and teachers of composition at the college level have done so; see, for example, Brooke, 1987; McGee, 1987; Murphy, 1989). I looked to the "socio" rather than the "psycho," to the workings of language, culture, and power in the lives of speakers and writers, and conceived of teacher response as socioanalysis. Response as socioanalysis assumed that traces of racial, class, and gender oppression would, at times, find their way into the stories children told.

Freire's (1985) notion of dialogue helped me elaborate what response as socioanalysis might entail. Within teacher-student dialogues, the teacher's role was to "propose problems about the codified existential situation in order to help learners arrive at a more and more critical view of their reality" (p. 55). Students come to these dialogues not empty, but filled with stories of the world. However, these stories are formed within oppressive social relations that bestow privileges on some individuals and groups, and on their stories. Freire's notion of dialogue insists on the use of student stories and the questioning of those stories. The first move validates the learner as a knowing person and makes available the learner's insights into the conditions of her existence (insights that may well challenge and teach the teacher). The second move, however, refuses to accept the learner's stories as given or final, and helps her to critically appraise them.

Habermas's (1970, 1984, 1987) and Young's (1990) work on communicative action helped specify what it was I would follow and/or question as I responded to children's texts. Habermas' theory of communication emphasizes the cognitive-instrumental, normative, and expressive functions of language. With any utterance (spoken or written), various claims are raised. In fact, any utterance *always* raises, explicitly or implicitly, at least three sorts of claims: claims as to what is true or effective (cognitive-instrumental claims), what is right (normative claims), and what a person's feelings, beliefs, and so forth, are (expressive or sincerity claims). In response to a speaker/writer's utterance, a hearer/reader evaluates these various claims, and accepts or questions one or more of the claims made with that utterance.

Following the child, as a conception of response, emphasizes conversations with children that focus on what does and does not work in their attempts at expression—in other words, teacher response would remain in the instrumental realm and focus on effectiveness. This is not necessarily an inappropriate teacher move in any given occasion for response, as long as we understand that this focus leaves unchallenged, *and therefore tacitly accepts*, other aspects of a text's content. When Graves (1983), for example, endorses a teacher's efforts to help a child improve his story on military weapons and killing by asking for more detail (pp. 120–123), he (like the teacher) is taking a position on the content of the story, even as he seems to ignore it. This is following the child, which, as Willinsky (1990) notes in his own response to this example of "appropriate" response in Graves, "seems a little odd in the case of an excited description of the damage the weapons of war can cause" (p. 49).

Habermas' work helped me conceptualize teacher resonse to children's texts by pointing to the various claims any utterance raises. In addition to responding to children's texts in ways that helped make them more effective, I also wanted to engage children in discussions of the moral and political aspects of their texts, in conversations about truth, and how their texts did and did not represent who they were and what they wanted to become.

The shift from following the child to socioanalysis is well-delineated with reference to Habermas' distinction between reflexive and nonreflexive learning.

> Non-reflexive learning takes place in action contexts in which implicitly raised theoretical (technical) and practical (ethical-political) validity claims are naively taken for granted and accepted or rejected without discursive consideration. Reflexive learning takes place through discourses in which we thematize practical validity claims that have become problematic or have been rendered problematic. (cited in Young, 1990, p. 42)

Following the child is partially committed to a vision of reflexive learning. It does engage children in discussions of technique. And in the context of traditional, teacher-dominated discourse, its emphasis on student voice and experience challenges the normative claim that teachers should talk and students listen. But in its conception of response to the content of children's texts, it remains nonreflexive, and ignores what their texts have to say about how it is we should live together and what it is we value as members of a classroom and society. Response as socioanalysis would aspire to reflexive learning. My students and I would critically examine the "traditionally given," and challenge claims embedded in the cultural material we worked with as we wrote our stories.

———

These were my beginnings—a commitment to artistic and political voice, a workshop architecture with spaces to write and share, and two evolving conceptions of teacher response to children's texts. With dreams of children writing themselves and their worlds on the page, and of me supporting and challenging their visions, I started teaching writing in Grace

Parker and Ruth Meyer's third grade classroom the last days of August. Grace and Ruth each taught half-time, Grace mornings and Ruth afternoons. I visited and talked with Ruth occasionally, but taught mornings, and spent most of my time that year with Grace. I taught 5 days a week, for approximately 45 minutes each day, but was at the school 2 to 3 hours each morning, and most of that in Grace's classroom—planning opening meetings, gathering materials, writing notes, typing children's stories, meeting with children who needed some special help, teaching, and researching. (See the appendix for full description of workshop schedule and length of study.)

Nothing we do goes as planned. Before I started this project, I had largely thought of myself as a teacher and a researcher, as if I were two different people at different times, or as if there would not be overlaps and conflicts among these roles in my day-to-day work. Teaching made demands that conflicted with research demands. And as I struggled—as a teacher—to understand and respond to the actions and texts of children in the classroom, the original focus of my research gave way to a new one. I began with an emphasis on my own teaching experiences. As for student experiences, I was interested in them only in relation to the teacher (me) and a teacher-manipulated environment. But children were also engaged in social relations with each other, and these social relations were extremely important for children's experiences and writing in my classroom. My research methods, as well as the focus of my research, were greatly influenced by aspects of my teaching and by my commitments as an educator.

Chapter 2

Teacher-Researcher Practice

I left the house with my 1-year-old son, John Jacob, on my shoulders, heading for a meeting with Bill Johnson, the principal at Clifford, at 11:00 AM. It would be my first official contact with the school, other than the phone call to set up the appointment. There were two ways for John Jacob and me to walk the four or five blocks to the school. One way took us up our street (mostly rental properties) and over to the school on a gently curved lane past well-kept lawns and houses—a fairly representative section of the predominantly white, middle-class neighborhood the school served. We took the other route, which was a little shorter.

We walked across the street, through a parking lot, and alongside the 8 or 9-foot wooden fence that separated a large trailer park from the well-kept lawns. We turned with the fence at an alley that ended near the school. The entrance to the trailer park opened onto the alley and faced the backsides of a liquor store and an old motel. The entrance offered the only look at the trailer park; otherwise the fence kept it hidden from view. I was always surprised at how close together the angled trailers were—just enough space, it seemed, to park a pick-up truck or car. The trailers were mostly white, dusty, some were peeling. There was no grass, only white stones and dirt, as far as I could tell. I knew a few children who lived here. They sometimes played with John Jacob and me on our front lawn.

The meeting with Bill went well. John Jacob sat quietly, and Bill and I decided I would meet with the teachers at Clifford the following week.

> I was consciously trying to present myself to Bill as someone who was a teacher. I told him I wanted to teach writing, that the legitimacy of my research depended on my actually teaching, since I wanted to write about it from that perspective. He was surprised when I said that

> I would teach every day for the entire year. He called it "ambitious" and then added that he meant it in a good way. (Fieldnotes, 5-25-89)

I talked with the Clifford teachers at their final staff meeting for the year. I told them I wanted to teach writing in someone's classroom for about 45 minutes every day, and that I wanted to write about what happened. I also told them that it would be up to the person I worked with to decide how much she or he wanted to be involved in the work.

Seven teachers wanted to talk with me about my project, and I met with each of them individually over the next week as they wrapped up their teaching for the year and straightened their rooms for the summer. I declined offers from several teachers who wanted me in their room, but could not promise me that I would have time each day to work with children on writing. The daily schedules of the fourth and fifth grade teachers seemed especially prohibitive this way. A few teachers had envisioned a sort of tutor role for me with children who had trouble with class writing assignments. One teacher asked me if I would like to help her in her writing workshop. She had been experimenting with workshop approaches for several years. I told her she had probably faced and resolved many of the problems and issues I was interested in learning and writing about. We agreed that we would talk to each other the following year about what we were trying to do.

I realized as I talked to the first several teachers that it was very important to me and my sense of this project that I have control of a classroom for a period of time each day. I wanted to be *the* writing teacher, even if the regular classroom teacher worked collaboratively with me in various ways. I decided to work with Grace even before we had finished talking.

> Grace told me that she was "stuck" in writing, that she had been able to get kids to enjoy writing and to write in response to story starters, but she didn't know what to do next. She said she wanted to have children talk to one another about their writing, but wasn't sure about setting it up. She was wondering how to manage all this. As I listened, I thought that this would be a good place to be. I will have enough autonomy as the writing teacher to set up a writing workshop, but Grace also wants to learn more about teaching the way I am going to try. She seems to have similar interests and concerns to me. It feels like we could learn a lot, since we are at similar places in our thinking. (Fieldnotes, 6-7-89)

I talked with Grace several times during the summer on the phone. She told me that, at the beginning, she wanted to watch what I was doing. Her primary interest, she said, was learning how to manage a program like the writing workshop. She said she had read Graves (1983) and

Calkins (1986) in masters classes she had taken, but still had trouble envisioning what such teaching would look like. She also told me that she would be job sharing with Ruth. We decided that she and Ruth would introduce me to the class on their first day of school, and that I would start up the workshop the following morning.

————

Grace and Ruth were going through the different schedules, rules, and routines for the class when I walked into the room. I waved to Grace and quickly sat down at a round table at the side of the room, near the door. I would do most of my conferencing with children at this round table.

Grace stood at the front of the room. There was a large green chalk board in the center of the front wall with bulletin boards on each side of it. Grace's desk was in the front corner, opposite me. Ruth was in the other far corner, near her desk. She was pointing to a bulletin board on the back wall, and telling the children about classroom jobs each of them would perform at different times throughout the year. There was another large chalkboard on the back wall, and what looked to be a portable, off-white closet next to it. The room had a small bathroom in the corner to my right and a bookshelf, cupboards, and a faucet and sink filled the wall behind me.

Soon after I arrived, Grace introduced me.

> I am sure I didn't sound too confident. It is not the kids—I do not feel easy talking to students with other adults around. I said that I was going to be their writing teacher, and that we wouldn't be working on handwriting, but on stories, poems, reports—I stumbled sort of here. I couldn't use words like "composition" to contrast handwriting. I probably will fumble like this a lot, not knowing the right words for third graders. I told them a little about the workshop routine before Grace took over again. (Fieldnotes, 8-29-89)

I started teaching the next day, and the day, and the month, and the year were harder than I had expected or wanted. I soon found myself fantasizing about pursuing a different project—maybe one in which I learned about writing and teaching writing by sitting in the library and reading books.

————

I had expected some difficulties getting the writing workshop off the ground and running. The workshop called for new participation structures, new "rights and obligations of participants with respect to who can say what, when, and to whom" (Cazden, 1986, p. 437; see also Philips, 1983). The opening meeting would be closest to traditional classroom lessons, with the discourse largely controlled by me, the teacher (Mehan, 1979, 1982). But writing time and sharing time called for discourse patterns breaking with the typical sequence of teacher initiation, student response, and teacher evaluation. During writing time, much classroom talk would take place among children with limited teacher surveillance. And sharing time replaced the teacher at the front of the room with the child-writer who reads books and solicits responses from students.

In other words, I expected confusion as the children and I attempted to do something new in the classroom. We brought old how-to knowledge to a situation in which I hoped to upset traditional procedures and rules. Furthermore, these children were working with two other teachers in the room—Grace and Ruth—for much longer periods than they spent with me. These teachers organized their lessons at least a little differently from each other, as well as differently from the writing workshop. Finally, given social class and ethnic differences, as well as individual differences, the children themselves brought diverse competencies and assumptions to their work with me on writing (Heath, 1983; Michaels, 1981). There would be plenty of occasions for confusion, as my students and I brought what we knew and were learning about how to participate in school from a variety of settings.

But this is a very friendly interpretation of possible sources of difficulty in the workshop. It assumes that everyone, more or less, is interested in doing things in these new ways but gets hung up when they use old knowledge in a new setting. It forgets conflict. It ignores that teachers and students sometimes take up adversarial roles. Children's "old knowledge" of school certainly includes knowledge of how to help things go smoothly, how to cooperate, but it also includes knowledge of how to disrupt, resist, engage the teacher in classroom warfare. If the writing workshop loosens the lid on tightly controlled classrooms, it loosens the lid on more than just repressed *positive* possibilities. If we assume that at least some children are alienated from school work (as in Everhart, 1983), and/or engaged in resistance to teacher authority and control (Willis, 1977; Connell et al., 1982), then loosening teacher control in the workshop may well promote an avoidance of writing and work, and increased—or at least continued—student attempts to subvert teacher authority. The workshop becomes a place, in a child's school history of alienated labor and teacher domination, for increased opportunities for rest, for avoiding work, for opposing the teacher, even as the teacher embraces a "gentle pedagogy" that avoids overt displays of teacher power (Hogan, 1989).

This was a tough class of children to work with, partly because a number of children actively resisted teachers in the classroom. You will get some sense of this in the chapters that follow. Ruth, a competent teacher with 7 years of teaching experience, tried (and failed) to get out of her teaching contract after struggling for little over a month with this group of children. Substitute teachers made a special point to walk over to my round table where I waited to teach writing, to tell me that this was one of the worst classes they had ever subbed in—one substitute teacher sharpened her evaluation by pointing out that she had worked in some of the toughest urban elementary schools around, and never had she met a more difficult group of children to handle. As I talked with other teachers in the building, I learned that the children in this and the other third grade class (taught by Samuel) were generally recognized as an extremely difficult group of children to teach. Samuel and Grace eventually attempted, with the support of the school's parent-teacher organization, to get another third grade classroom at Clifford, in order to reduce class size (Samuel had 28 students; Grace, 27). They were unsuccessful, though an additional fourth grade teacher was hired for this group of children the following year.

I faced confusion and conflict in the writing workshop. The 1st month was especially frustrating and emotionally draining.

> This is getting a little tiring, feeling so frustrated and depressed after teaching (what teaching?). I can't seem to get done the things I hope to. I am angry. James, Suzanne, Robert, Bruce, Ken are getting me angry. They are testing me. And I am feeling humiliated in front of Grace. (Fieldnotes, 9-11-89)

I felt vulnerable in front of Grace, and in front of the children as well. I worried about what this meant for my teaching and my students' experiences in the classroom.

> When I taught junior high, there were one or two classes each year I didn't feel good with—for some reason, sixth period my 2nd year sticks in my head. I didn't do the same things with that class that I did with other classes, because I didn't feel I could trust them. I think I felt too vulnerable in front of them, I kept a distance. The problem is that I am feeling this way about this class. I feel vulnerable in front of them.
>   The bigger problem is that I won't take risks with them. I won't do the special things that maybe would really get them interested. We're tied in a bad circle. I begin trying to do interesting things. For whatever reasons, the students (some) don't cooperate, don't make me feel they are with me. I then adjust, and my adjustment is to worry more about making children behave. This of course backfires, and causes some to resist more; others, who weren't resisting before get sick of me talk-

ing about people misbehaving. Pretty soon, we're sick of each other. Obviously, I'm the one who has to bust out of this. I need to figure out how. (Fieldnotes, 9-15-89)

In early October, I had a particularly bad day. The confusion got to me.

Rajesh probably came and talked to me four or five times during writing time. He got on my nerves. One time he said he didn't know what to put down on his sheet of Ideas for Topics. Another time he said he didn't know what to write about. I felt as if he was always tugging on my arm as I tried to help other children. I remember Rajesh and how I felt because I usually enjoy him so much. I didn't today. (Fieldnotes, 10-2-89)

And the conflict got to me.

I said that it felt like they were fighting me. The word "fight" must be too vivid or exciting. James sat in the back of the room, saying over and over, "We're fighting you, we're fighting you," swinging his fists in the air. (Fieldnotes, 10-2-89)

The emotional, physical, and intellectual demands caught up with me. I did not have it within me to go to school the next day. I talked to Grace in the morning on the phone, and she suggested we talk that afternoon after she finished teaching. We met in the teachers' lounge, which was empty. She gave me a letter written in blue magic marker.

Tim,

Twenty of your students are ready to fly with the writers' workshop, seven are not. Unfortunately, these seven will set the tone for the others.

Tailor make the WW to meet the needs of these seven. They need lots of structure, clear directions and expectations, one task to deal with at a time, quiet. They are easily distracted and fall off task easily. Gradually, ease into a full blown WW.

There are many activities I'd like to try with this group, but I've put them on hold until they are ready. Otherwise I'd be pulling out my hair and downing bottles of Pepto.

The issues of movement and noise will take care of themselves once the seven have a handle on the WW.

I don't expect you to be a clone of me. As long as the kids are learning, being cooperative and you're having fun—I'm okay. But are you having fun yet?

The teaching of writing is frustrating enough. Never enough time to conference with each child. To complicate matters even more, you're dealing with 27 kids, 7 of which have special needs.

It's the reality of teaching. Not all programs are easily imple-
mented. You nip and tuck at it (tailor make it) until it fits.

WW is a wonderful program. You have a wonderful way with
kids. Let's put the program to work our way first. By spring, it will be
the real thing.

Grace

In her letter, Grace gave an analysis of what she thought had been
happening in the workshop: seven students were not handling it very
well. She also shared her own teacherly response to this class, which was
to not do certain activities (presumably less "structured") because she
believed her students were not ready for them. She related her own version of what I had been going through: "pulling out my hair and downing bottles of Pepto."

I talked with Grace about what she meant by "special needs." Her
use of the term had little to do with psychological or intellectual defi-
ciency on the children's part. She meant what she said at the beginning,
that these particular children, in her opinion, needed "lots of structure,"
"one task at a time," and "quiet." She saw these adjustments as at odds
with a sort of official version of the workshop—"the real thing"—I was
trying to set up. Grace asserted that seven specific children needed
something a little different from what "the writing workshop program"—
as interpreted by her in her own readings of Graves and Calkins, and
through her interactions with me—offered. But she also believed that the
workshop was a good thing to do, and that these children would eventually function well within it.

I should note that Graves and Calkins are quite clear about there
being no one right way to do writing workshops. Their books are
filled with stories of many versions that they applaud for their respon-
siveness to children and for how they draw on the particular strengths
of individual teachers. Still, a basic assumption of these approaches is
that if you allow children to write, they will do so (and, it seems, not
do other sorts of things, like throw paper or hit people). This assumption is tied to Graves' and Calkins' critiques of traditional approaches
to the teaching of writing, which actually produce resistance to writing
as they "take the control away from children and place unnecessary
road blocks in the way of their intentions" (Graves, 1983, p. 4). Grace,
at different times in the year, questioned the amount of control that
workshop approaches granted children. Similar to Delpit (1988), she
believed that this control actually allowed some children to avoid (or
prevented them from) learning what they needed to learn. Grace was
also concerned with things going smoothly in the classroom, and

increased levels of student autonomy tended to make things jagged and noisy. Her letter expresses, if faintly, some of these doubts and beliefs.

Grace's letter was extremely important to me that Tuesday afternoon—not for its insight into the needs of children and its critical response to workshop approaches, but for the support, affirmation, and solidarity it offered. Grace recognized my struggle ("are you having fun yet?"), affirmed my work with children in the room ("you have a wonderful way with kids"), and expressed her willingness to work with me in the future ("Let's [let *us*] put this program to work *our* way"). Her offer came at a crucial time, and I gratefully accepted.

The workshop routines and norms, and my work there, did not change drastically. I still did the planning (sometimes in consultation with Grace), conducted the opening meetings, worked with children at the round table—in other words, I was still largely responsible for the shape and content of the workshop. But Grace became an important part of the day-to-day experiences of the children and me there. She helped me most during writing time. She usually circulated around the room, helping children write or *remember* they were supposed to be writing (or reading or conferencing). Grace and I discussed what we saw happening and what we should do about various children and problems in the few minutes we had around the edges of teaching and family demands— sometimes we talked a little longer over lunch, but not as often as we would have liked.

Our relationship was transformed under the pressures of working with children in new and demanding ways.

> Grace gave me a note to read, written in blue magic marker. I told her how I tried to respect what teachers knew, but that deep inside I must have thought that I really had learned how to do this stuff in graduate school. I didn't expect it to be this hard. (Inside, that morning while I was thinking about talking to Grace, I had been humbled, and it freed me. Maybe this was necessary. I would start over, with more respect for how hard this was and for what Grace knew. Maybe I would learn more.) (Fieldnotes, 10-3-89)

Grace's help allowed me to become *a* teacher in the classroom, rather than *the* teacher. Her participation in the workshop, especially during writing time, allowed me the luxury of talking with children about their work at the round table with fewer distractions and responsibilities for the rest of the class. She allowed me to become more of a student of writing and its instruction, a researcher. I turn to this aspect of my work at Clifford in the remainder of this chapter.

But before I do, I want to note that Grace's participation in the workshop did not suddenly remove confusion or conflict from the room. She joined the struggles I had been experiencing more or less alone—or, more accurately, she joined the struggles my students and I were experiencing as we tried to go about teaching and writing in a writing workshop.

———

Even as I labored to negotiate my teacher role in relation to Grace and our students, I struggled with my broader role as a teacher-researcher. Although I had written about my classroom as a "philosophical laboratory" (Berthoff, 1987) in early proposals, and my plans for data collection were fairly well tuned to the goal of critically examining the intersection of theory and practice in my teaching, it was not until I began this work that I seriously considered some of the conflicts and issues that attended actually pursuing teacher and researcher roles simultaneously. In what follows, I discuss the main conflicts I encountered, and then describe how I responded to these conflicts in my day-to-day research.

Four conflicts shaped my work as a teacher-researcher at Clifford. These conflicts originated in:

1. Divergent teaching and research demands for my attention while I taught;
2. The influence of emotional responses to my teaching on my notewriting;
3. Questions as to the content and function of fieldnotes in a teacher research project; and
4. The need to narrow my research focus and data collection without privileging some children over others in my day-to-day work as a teacher.

The first conflict arose out of demands for my attention in my everyday work as a teacher-researcher. Being a teacher put demands on where and when I could look at things while I was teaching. Whereas a more traditional classroom researcher can sit at the back of the room and make decisions as to when and where to attend, my vision and attention were often tied to my activity and responsibility as a teacher. A researcher, for example, might purposely ignore John biting Suzanne in order to listen carefully to a peer conference between Carol and Maya, but a teacher will feel he cannot. At issue was my ability, as a teacher-researcher, to engage in data collection as a type of progressive problem-solving (Erickson, 1986), in which what I attended to (and then wrote about in my fieldnotes) represented a *deliberate* process of gathering evidence to support and challenge emerging theories (Glaser & Strauss, 1967; Hammersly & Atkinson, 1983). I often felt more reactive than proactive in my decisions of when and where I would "look" in the classroom. The problem of "bounded rationality"—simplifying complexity because of limits of information-processing capacity (Simon, 1957)—takes on a socially constructed twist here. I was bounded, as an interpretive researcher attempting to describe and understand a complex classroom situation, not only by processing capacity, but also socially, in my role as the teacher.

A second conflict pitted my emotional responses to my teaching experiences against research demands that I write fieldnotes each day as an important source of data, and as part of an ongoing process of data analysis and methodological problem solving. My emotional responses to teaching, especially how well or badly I thought things went, affected my notewriting. At the extremes of magnificent and devastating experiences as a teacher in the classroom, it often seemed harder for me to get myself to write fieldnotes. If things went well, I would rather celebrate and talk about it with friends; if badly, I wanted to forget about what happened rather than dwell on, relive for the purposes of notetaking, what had caused me distress in the first place. I usually overcame these responses, but I often noted how depressed I was, how tired, how my feelings discouraged notewriting.

This is not to suggest that the only reason I resisted writing fieldnotes was because of my teaching—sometimes, like most interpretive researchers, I simply did not feel up to the intellectual and physical labor writing notes demanded. I am also not suggesting that more traditional researchers are never depressed or tired or giddy, or that such feelings, in my case, only related to my teaching and not other aspects of my life. My point is that as a teacher-researcher, I had a certain emotional investment in what happened in the classroom that more traditional researchers would usually not have, and that this investment affected data collection, in as much as it made writing fieldnotes more or less difficult for me to do.

One way I attempted to help myself overcome resistance to writing fieldnotes was to experiment with various ways of recording them. I began the year typing my notes at a computer. A couple of weeks into my work (and remember, I was struggling in my teaching here), I bought an artsy blank book with an illustration every few pages and short quotations from "real" authors for inspiration.

> I wanted to have an inviting place to write my notes—we'll see if this thing does the trick. I wasn't planning on getting anything this gim-

micky, but the other blank books I saw were either too small or too
impressive and expensive. I wouldn't want to write in them. (Fieldnotes, 9-15-89)

At the bottom of this very first page was a Jack London quotation:
"You can't wait for inspiration. You have to go after it with a club." Just the
sort of thing a slightly battered teacher, looking for a safe, peaceful place
to write, needed. For most of the fall, I went back and forth between hand-
written notes in this blank book, and typed ones on my computer, not very
pleased or comfortable with either. After Christmas, I found some inex-
pensive, large, hard-covered blank books (no illustrations or quotations)
and wrote my fieldnotes in them consistently through the end of the year.

The third conflict I encountered in my roles as teacher and
researcher concerned the content and function of my fieldnotes: What
sort of notes would I write? When I wrote fieldnotes for my first day of
teaching, I already realized that research goals of description—"to capture the slice of life" in order to provide "the clues that you begin to put
together to make analytical sense of what you study" (Bogdan & Biklen,
1982, pp. 84, 86)—were in conflict with more teacherly goals of reflection and planning that I might press my notes toward. After three pages
of mostly descriptive material, I wrote:

> Ideas for teaching tomorrow keep intruding—for instance, I just dazed
> off and was thinking that I need to express to the kids tomorrow that
> the workshop is a chance to write about things they care about, think
> about things they want to think about. (Fieldnotes, 8-30-89)

I continued for a page and a half, before pulling myself back to
description with "Back to notes." Teacher reflections were often sparked
by my attempts to describe what happened in class that day. But as a
teacher, I often felt the need to move beyond description to an evaluation of what happened, in order to formulate for myself what needed to
be done in the future.

Again, I do not want to suggest some absolute break with what I
faced as a teacher-researcher and the problems other interpretive
researchers encounter. The content of qualitative fieldnotes includes both
descriptive and reflective material. Descriptive material attempts to record
details of the people, conversations, physical setting, events, activities,
and researcher behavior that make up the research setting. Reflective
material expresses the "more subjective side of the researcher's journey,"
and contains speculations, hunches, impressions, as well as methodological notes for future research in the field (Bogdan & Biklen, 1982, p. 86).

Any interpretive researcher, then, faces decisions of balance between these different sorts of material. However, for me the problem was intensified because the initial questions guiding my research emphasized investigating how teaching writing was experienced by me, the teacher. (See appendix for discussion of beginning research questions.) In other words, the reflective material, in which I mulled over teacher problems and how I was feeling, was an extremely important part of the study as I began my work. At the same time I knew I needed rich descriptions of classroom life in the workshop in order to investigate what was happening there and what this meant to other participants. My goals for the study went beyond teacher autobiography. I wanted to study what happened in the classroom—not just to me— when I tried to teach writing in a writing workshop. I wanted to ground the teacherly issues and problems I was facing in a plausible account of workshop life.

"Teacherly" notes, then, were important both as a tool for improving teacher practice through reflection, and as a record of my thinking and experience in the classroom. "Researcherly" notes, focused on description, also remained important. In an ideal situation in which I would have unlimited time and motivation to write fieldnotes, I could pursue both sorts of notes without conflict. But in the actual situation I faced, the two were often in competition for my time and effort, and any act of notetaking represented conscious and unconscious choices of emphasis.

A fourth and final conflict arose as I thought about ways to narrow my research focus in order to gain a depth of data and begin the gradual process of confirming, revising, and disproving various assertions I was formulating in relation to what was happening in the workshop, and what problems my students and I faced there in our work. A common way to focus data collection and analysis in studies of classrooms is to eventually identify and concentrate on a limited number of children. These children become key informants as well as foci for observation and collection of documents. I considered this move throughout the year, but could not shake the worry that such a research commitment would also entail a teacher commitment—that is, that the goal of learning more about particular children for research purposes would in some way affect my teacherly decisions, and ultimately benefit some children over others.

My discussions of the other conflicts I encountered have focused on how teaching constrained or complicated my research efforts. But here, the problem was my research affecting my teaching. I was aware that my research goals sometimes pushed back on my teaching. For example, after a discussion with Grace about how to manage writing conferences with individual children while keeping the rest of the class on track, I noted:

> If I weren't doing research in the workshop, I probably wouldn't conference with children at the round table at the side of the room so often, but do it at the children's desks, moving around the room. I feel the tug as a researcher to stay close to the tape recorder. (Fieldnotes, 12-13-89)

I was concerned about a similar research "tug" toward certain children, and not others. The writing workshop, especially during writing time, was a fairly open place in which children and teachers made decisions to do this and not that—to work with this person and not that person—on an almost moment-to-moment basis. As a teacher, I worried about more or less unconscious preferences I might be expressing for certain children in these decisions. As a result, within the 1st month of my teaching, I created a weekly schedule that ensured that I talked regularly with each individual child in the room. A research focus on certain children may have encouraged me to attend to some children more than others, even as I consciously sought to work with children according to their needs (and not my own).

By early November, I had come to a way of proceeding in my work that responded to these conflicts. This response had two aspects: a daily routine of data collection, and a relative emphasis on writing conferences to focus the study.

I started collecting what I called "packets of data" each day. At least four types of data made up my packet of data—I would have *teacher planning notes*; *fieldnotes*; an *audiotape* of the day's teacher-student writing conferences, as well as our opening meeting and sharing time; and photocopies of any *children's stories* I came in contact with that day, in conferences or whole-class sessions.

Collecting packets did several things for me. The collection of audiotapes, children's writing, and planning notes each day eased my concerns about my ability to capture rich detail and important events in my fieldnotes (because I attended to certain things and not others, because I was too depressed to write a lot, because I wanted to use my notes to figure out a pedagogical problem, etc.). What I did not cover with fieldnotes could be partially filled in, if need be, with audiotapes and other data. And, of course, the collection of four sorts of data rather than only fieldnotes gave me multiple sources to draw from to better understand what was happening in the room. Children's writing and the audiotapes, for example, were less constrained in what they "looked at" than I was in my role as teacher in the classroom.

As I realized that my daily data collection would support my research interests, I became more comfortable with using my fieldnotes for reflections on my teaching. And the fact that I photocopied children's writing that I came in contact with each day proved crucial to these reflections. Originally, I had planned to collect classroom sets of children's writing at periodic intervals. But without a child's text in front of me as I wrote notes, it was difficult to write about what happened and what I was thinking about as I responded to the child and her text, even with an audiotape of our conversation. Having children's texts also allowed me to begin the work of connecting writing conference talk with the writing children did in the room.

My daily methods served my research and teacher interests fairly well. I was collecting the sorts of data that would allow me to write plausible accounts of what was happening, as well as using my notewriting and the data I collected to reflect on and inform my teaching practice.

My methods also served a more or less explicit research focus. From the beginning, a teacher experience I wanted to write about was responding to children's writing. My packets of data were well suited to such a focus. Each day, I had fieldnotes, photocopies of children's stories, and audiotapes that addressed this experience. I had solved the problem of focus (at least temporarily) not by looking to particular children, but by attending closely to a fairly compact event and location—the writing conferences with children at the round table at the side of the room.

In the end, responding to children's texts did not turn out to be the primary focus of my work and writing, even though it remained important. My eventual focus did, however, emerge out of my experiences with children in writing conferences. In my conversations with children about their writing, I began to learn about the importance of peers to children's writing processes and texts. I learned that in order to understand and respond to their writing, I often needed to know about social relations among children.

———

For all the concern I expressed as a teacher for student experience and voice, I showed little interest in children's voices in my early plans for research. My earliest memos and proposals show a strong emphasis on *my* experiences as a teacher in setting up a workshop and responding to children's writing, and do not even include student interviews. Gradually, children's experiences and problems became more important to my research. But even then, I thought of children's experiences in relation to me and a teacher-manipulated environment, and ignored influences of peers on children's experiences.

For example, in a proposal for funding I wrote in early November, 1989, I said that the following three questions would guide my research:

1. What problems and difficulties do children encounter as they attempt to become authors in classrooms?
2. What pedagogical problems and difficulties arise when teachers take seriously the notion of student ownership?
3. What is involved in establishing and sustaining a classroom environment that supports children writers?

In my discussion of the sorts of difficulties children were likely to encounter in their writing, I emphasized authority relations between teachers and students and the pervasiveness of evaluation in schools as situational constraints that might undermine children's efforts to take control of their writing in writing workshops. In other words, I looked to teacher-student relations as an important determinant of children's experiences in the classroom. I wrote that "part of the problem for children writing in classrooms . . . is exactly that they are writing in classrooms in which teachers and students take up certain roles and relations with one another" (Proposal, 11–89).

In order to investigate children's experiences more thoroughly, I added interviews of children, by outside researchers, to the research methods I was already pursuing. I attribute the absence of interviewing before this proposal to two factors. The relative emphasis on my own teaching experience at the beginning of the project made data collection on children's experience less crucial. But more importantly, I had considered writing conferences to be important sources of information on children's experiences in the workshop.

And they were. My conversations with children about their texts often functioned much like interviews: I asked children questions about their writing—how they did it, what special problems they were having, why they did what they did—so that I could understand how they were attempting to solve writing problems, and support them in their efforts. These conversations were audiotaped, and provided a valuable source of data on children's writing and how they thought about it. But, by the time of this proposal, I recognized that, at least for some children, I may have been one of the problems or difficulties they were experiencing in the writing workshop, and that students may very well be reluctant to talk about problems they were having with the teacher when the teacher was also the interviewer. I planned for colleagues to conduct extended interviews of children toward the end of the school year. I conceived of these interviews as occasions to explore children's perceptions of writing and our writing workshop, with some attention to students' relations with Grace and me.

As I worked with these children across the year—as well as watched them play on the playground, vote for student council representatives, decide who to sit by in the cafeteria—I began to pay attention to peer relations in the workshop. I realized that peers were extremely important to—and not necessarily in positive ways—the experiences of children in the workshop and their writing. Several teachers in the building told me that children from the trailer park formed their own subculture in the school, and tended to only have friends from the trailer park. From my observations, this division seemed largely repeated in the workshop. Lines did not appear to be drawn by race. The four African-American children in our classroom and one whose parents were from India did not form a subgroup—each of them worked and played primarily with white children within gender boundaries.

I noted patterns of association among children that divided them along gender and social class lines (if we take the fence separating the children living in the trailer park from those living in the surrounding suburban community as a rough social-class line). In the workshop, girls worked with girls, and boys with boys; and the boys and girls who lived in the trailer park were at the bottom of informal peer hierarchies of status and power in the classroom, although there were several children who did not live there who also occupied similar positions.

Toward the end of my teaching at Clifford, and then into my analysis and writing, this aspect of children's experiences and writing in the workshop became more and more central to my research.

In late March and April, I began developing interview questions that would help me understand the sense children made of our writing workshop. I wanted children to talk about what they thought typically happened in various parts of the workshop, and how they felt about what happened, as well as comment on particular incidents or aspects of the workshop and their work that caused them trouble. There were questions about their relations with me and Grace, as well as their relations with other children. Children's responses to questions about their relations with other children were extremely important for my later analysis and writing. Some of the questions used to explore peer relations were:

Who are the people in the class you like to be with and work with? Why? Are there people you don't like to be with and work with? Why?

What usually happened in conferences with classmates? What sorts of things would they say? Did you always use their advice? Why or why not? What did you say in conferences? Did you like peer conferences? Have you ever had bad experiences in conferences with classmates?

What was sharing time like? How did you feel about it? Are there people in class you would rather not read your stories in front of? Who? Why?

Did children ever tease one another during the writing workshop? When/how/why did they do it? Did students ever use writing to tease one another or hurt someone else's feelings? How did they do it? Why is that "teasing?"

Who are the popular children in class? Why are they popular? Who are the unpopular children? Why are they unpopular?

In May, I arranged for three colleagues to conduct 1- to 1½-hour interviews with all but three of the children in the classroom. I instructed my colleagues to emphasize to the children that the purpose of the interviews was to learn about what *children* thought of the writing workshop, with the goal of making workshops better in the future. The interviews were audiotaped, and the tapes were transcribed early that summer.

One of the first things I did after my teaching ended was to read through the transcripts of children's interviews, paying particular attention to children's responses that commented on peer relations within the room. In the beginning, I concentrated on children who were at the extremes of the informal peer hierarchies I had observed. My hunch was that the workshop afforded rather dramatically different experiences for different children, depending on who they were in relation to other children. Gradually, I looked to other children's interviews for commonalities and contrasts, and began reading fieldnotes and listening to audiotapes in order to investigate what peer relations meant for children's experiences in the room, and how they affected children's writing processes and texts.

I also began examining children's texts. I drew on the literary theories of Bakhtin (1981, 1986) and Kristeva (1986) to analyze children's texts in relation to the social contexts of their production. For Bakhtin, texts respond to preceding and anticipated texts and are sensitive to audience and social context. Texts are "dialogic," in that they are responsive to others and to their texts. Kristeva (1986), an early interpreter of

Bakhtin in the West, characterized the dialogic nature of text in terms of horizontal and vertical relations.

> The word's status is thus defined horizontally (the word in text belongs to both writing subject and addressee) as well as vertically (the word in text is oriented towards an anterior or synchronic literary corpus). (p. 37)

Any text is written in relation to some audience. That audience shapes the content and form of the text—the text "belongs" to both the author and audience. But texts also draw on and anticipate other texts. In my analyses, I did interpretations of children's texts where peers (not only teachers) were important audiences, and in which children drew not only on their conversations with teachers and their readings of books, but also the words, meanings, and values of their peer culture to construct their texts. In other words, I placed young writers in a social context in which peers were important audiences and sources of material, in order to investigate how peer culture intersected with the official work of the writing workshop.

My work as a teacher-researcher developed throughout the project. When I began, I called myself a teacher-researcher, but the term meant little more to me than the same person embracing two different roles. The development of my teacher-researcher practice was characterized by the progressive integration of my teacher and researcher roles. The activities and content of my work increasingly reflected both teacher and researcher demands and commitments.

In the beginning, I separated my teaching and research activities. Setting up the tape recorder, photocopying children's stories, writing fieldnotes at night—these were research activities I pursued in addition to my activities as a teacher. By the time I started collecting daily packets of data in November, my research and teaching activities had become more integrated. I used my notewriting for descriptive purposes, but also to think about my teaching and future action. I knew the audiotapes and photocopies of children's stories were essential for later analyses, but they also became essential for day-to-day assessments of what was happening and what to do about it. My research methods became part of my teaching methods, part of the movement from action to thought to action that I brought to my work with children.

By spring, not just the activities, but also the objects or contents of my teacher and researcher activities had begun to converge. In my teaching, I had a problem, and that problem became an important focus for my research and writing. The problem was reading, understanding, and responding to children's texts, when the meanings and functions of those texts were at least partially dependent on a peer culture to which I had limited access.

Chapter 3

Student Intention and Relations

James caught my attention quickly. I knew him by name after the first day of the workshop.

> James is going to be trouble for me—I didn't handle things well today. During writing time, after I explained that the children could choose what they wanted to write about, James first told me he didn't have anything to write about, then that he was going to write about vomit (other children snickered when he said this), and finally that he needed a new sheet of paper because he had messed the other one up. He approached me later and said that he didn't like writing. My response: "Well you are going to do some writing in here." Nice guy-understanding, patient, eager to learn about and help children. I need to get more sleep. (Fieldnotes, 8-30-89)

You might say James awoke me rather abruptly from my dreams of children writing themselves onto the page and into a community of authors. James also served notice that he was a force to be reckoned with in the classroom, both in his relationship with me as the teacher, and in his relationships with other children in the room. Among the boys, James was at the top of the pecking order, and commanded high status and influence among them. Of course, I did not know this then.

James (or rather, James and I) found something to write about the next day before class. Grace had asked me to come with her to get the children from gym class. As Grace and the gym teacher worked to quiet the children down and get them into a line, I realized that I was surprised and disappointed that children still had to get in lines and be absolutely quiet (though it seldom happened). I had not taught in schools for several years, and I guess I had assumed they had changed while I was gone.

Kurt and James interrupted my musings. They were arguing about Kurt's placement at the beginning of the line. Kurt claimed that he was supposed to be the line leader; James, that Kurt had led the line the day before from art, so someone else should be the line leader. I entered their conversation, partly to disrupt such a serious discussion of what I considered an arbitrary school procedure. I questioned Kurt as to whether he really, really was the line leader or not. James seemed to have caught on that I was playing, and soon was calling Kurt an imposter, and then a fake line leader. At the end of the year, James still remembered the origins of his first story:

> He [Kurt] said "I'm the line leader" and I go "No he's not, he's a fake line leader." And then I, then I looked at his colors [reference to University of Alabama sweatshirt Kurt was wearing] and I go "The fake line leader from Alabama." And Mr. Lensmire goes "Yeah, maybe you could write a story about that," and I did, and I put Kurt as the main character. (Interview, 5-24-90)

James soon enlisted a third boy from the class, Ken, as a collaborator on the piece, and they could be seen working together most days in the workshop. James often kneeled in his seat, leaning over across Ken's desk top as they worked. They seldom asked for help from Grace or me. I stopped in one day to see how things were going.

> I bent down by them, and Ken asked James if they should let me see a certain part of their story. James said, "He can read it." I didn't read the whole story, only to the middle of the page where the female and male lead characters meet on a train in the dining car. The next line said something like: "Then they went to bed." The "they" was Kurt and another character named after someone in the class—Lisa. I asked them if that was the part. They said yes. I asked if their story was like a James Bond movie (I was thinking of their spies and romantic liaisons, but didn't say this), and they said no, and seemed confused by the question. I got up and walked away.
>
> Later, I saw them in the front of the room with Grace. She had their paper in her hands and I saw her write something on their paper. (Fieldnotes, 9-15-89)

James and Ken later decided to publish the story, and they shared their typed and illustrated book with the class toward the end of November. Just before they were supposed to share, they came to me in a panic—they could not find their book. Soon, Ken had the contents of his desk on the floor as he looked for the book. James told me that I must have lost it; he was holding me responsible. I was surprised at how desperate and engaged they seemed. Usually, James was "cool"—a word used by other children to describe James and his friends in interviews—

distant, somewhat aloof, above showing too much visible emotion or interest in school activities. They finally found their book at the back table where Ken had worked the day before to finish the illustrations. They walked to the front of the room.

James sat in the author's chair, and Ken stood behind him and to his left with his hand resting on the back of the chair. They were cool again: James seemed at ease in the author's chair, arms resting on the sides, looking over the class. Ken had put on sunglasses with mirror frames. James read to a classroom audience that was unusually attentive and settled (at least as he began to read). James would read the text of one or two pages, and then pause to hold up the book so that his classmates could see the illustrations. When he held up the book for others to see, he often commented about the text or illustrations (Ken joined him on two occasions). He soon had large numbers of the class laughing and calling out responses to his reading and commentary. The text of their story—along with selected illustrations from their book—follows:

The Fake Line Leader from Alabama

Kurt called his boss. His boss said, "Your are going to Michigan to be a line leader. Mustn't tell anyone your name."

On the train to Michigan he saw a woman.

He sat down for dinner and the woman came up to him and said, "Is this seat taken?"

He said, "No," so she sat down. She said, "Hello, my name is Lisa," and he said, "My name is Kurt."

So they had dinner together—sushi with hot fudge sauce. The next morning they were in Michigan. When he got off the train he called his boss. His boss' name is Robert.

Kurt said, "Hello, Robert."
"Are you in Michigan?" Robert asked. Kurt said yes and Robert said, "Now you have to go to Clifford School."

"Wait a minute. You never said anything about going anywhere but Michigan. But you're the boss, so bye." So he went to get a taxi, but there was not any left.

So he walked and saw hippies. They said, "Would you like to get a hair cut?"

Kurt meets Lisa

Kurt's Mohawk

Kurt said, "OK," and he got a Mohawk and he had to stay on the street for the night until the Mohawk was gone. When the haircut was gone he was at the school. When he went into the school he called his boss. His boss said, "Go to Mrs. P's class." So when he found Mrs. P's class he saw Lisa. They were getting ready for lunch. Kurt went to Lisa and said, "Remember me?"

Lisa said, "Yes, come to lunch with me." So they went to lunch and had sushi with hot fudge sauce.

Kurt phones his boss

After lunch, Kurt called his boss. His boss said, "Did you see Lisa?"

"How did you know?"

"She is my other agent."

So on the train to Alabama they sat down for dinner and had sushi with hot fudge sauce. After dinner Kurt said, "I really don't like sushi with hot fudge sauce."

"I don' either," said Lisa.

When they got off at Alabama Lisa said, "Come to my house. I will cook you something good."

The End

James commented twice, during his performance, on problems with the typing I had done for their book. Once to say that what I had originally typed throughout the book as "Rubert" was supposed to be "Robert," and a second time to say that I had omitted a word. His comments were: "Mr. Lensmire typed it wrong. It says Robert," and later, "'Would you like to get a hair cut . . . a *free* hair cut.' Mr. Lensmire typed that one too" (Audiotape, 11-28-89; quotations in this section come from 11-28-89 tape).

James performed and interpreted *The Fake Line Leader from Alabama*, while most other children who shared in front of class simply read their texts. He spoke with energy and expression, and children responded overtly to his intonation and pitch, especially in his voice characterizations of Kurt. For example, after the hippies gave Kurt a Mohawk, James read Kurt's line in the illustration—"Oh no my hair!"— with a high pitch and breathy quality, and stretched out the word "hair" so that it reminded me of how cartoon characters stretch out "I'm falling" as they drop from a plane or a cliff to the earth. Loud laughter followed. And when James narrated the reunion of Kurt with Lisa at Clifford school, he read, "Remember me?" with an exaggerated rise in pitch on "me" to the seeming delight of his classmates.

James also found humor in the execution of one of Ken's illustrations. After reading about Kurt's third phone call to his boss, James commented on the size of Kurt in the illustration. In an earlier illustration (not included above), Kurt appears to be about the same size as the phone booth, but in the later one he is much smaller. James said, "He's on the phone. Ken kinda got, kinda shrunk him." Ken did not appear upset by this comment, and smiled as the class laughed. (However, the comment seems to have spurred a revision of the illustration which I accidently discovered when looking at two different photocopies I had made of their book—one on the day they shared it in November, and another I had made at the end of the year. The later version has Kurt slightly taller than the phone booth in both illustrations.)

But some of the loudest responses from the class, including laughter and student comments to each other and the authors, occurred when James and Ken discussed illustrations that implicated girls in the class. The first such response came when James showed the class the title page of *The Fake Line Leader*. The title page featured two people—a female and a male. The male figure is about half as tall as the female figure. When James displayed the title page for his classmates, he said, "Lisa is the *big* one." Later, when commenting on an illustration of Mrs. P's class, James and Ken gave names to figures in the illustration who were not named anywhere in the text of their story. More specifically, they said that the drawings were of girls from the class. Their comments provoked a loud response.

JAMES: (pointing at illustration) There's, there's, um, there's people in the class.

KEN: This one's Sharon (some laughter) and, um, what's the other one?

JAMES: Yeah, this one's Sharon and this one, this one is Suzanne. (Followed by laughter, general hubbub, student comments such as "Let me see, let me see" and "A nice green face"—one character's face was green in illustration.)

James seemed unsure, at first, about what to say about the illustration. Ken helped him out by suggesting one person in the illustration, and James followed up on Ken's lead. The two collaborated, again, in their response to student questions that followed the presentation of their book. Paul asked James and Ken, "How did you think of the story? That would have been hard for me." James responded that they first thought of the people, and that once they had the people, they just thought of the story. Suzanne, one of the girls identified as in the illustration of Mrs. P's class, followed this question up with one about consistency in the story.

SUZANNE: But I don't get it. The boss said do not tell anyone his name and then, then Kurt told Lisa that.

LENSMIRE: That's one of the jokes, right?

JAMES: That was one of the jokes because he, because he likes her so much that he forgot (student laughter, talking; one child said "Ooooo" with rising pitch, as if surprised or pretending to be surprised at revelation of Kurt's desire).

KEN: Yeah, they get married at the end. (Volume of laughter and talk increases.)

Ken's comment and the class' response ended sharing time, both because we were running out of time, and because sharing time had broken down into a number of conversations and some shouting. I quickly walked to the front of the room, and gave instructions over the excited talk and movement of children in the room, to put away writing folders and get ready for lunch. A number of children continued to talk about *The Fake Line Leader from Alabama* as they left for the cafeteria a few minutes later.

My story about the writing and sharing of James and Ken's book foreshadows several points—about who James was and what he was about in the classroom—that I develop later in the chapter. One is that James saw himself as *the funny person* in the workshop, and that the objects of his humor were often found in his immediate surroundings— other children, teachers, classroom situations. Another is that James and his friends often included classmates' names as the names of characters in their fiction, and that these inclusions were informed by existing social relations among children. Below, I comment on a few of the ways that James and Ken's writing and sharing responded to the particular social context within which they worked, by discussing the social origins of their story, the influence of teacher interventions, and the function of heterosexual meanings in their text.

———

James and Ken's text had very "social" origins (beyond social origins in shared language, conceptions of story and particular genres, etc.). Kurt and James had argued about who should be first in line. Their argument assumed a social (school) practice—lining up to walk back to class—in which they were, at the moment, participating. I joined their conversation at least partly to disrupt their seriousness but also to poke fun at that school practice. When James called Kurt a fake line leader, I responded that James might want to write a story about that. His comment had suggested something like a spy/secret agent story or maybe a story about an impostor—in my fieldnotes that night I wrote that I might want to help James find news stories about impostors.

My response to James' comment—you could write a story about that—makes sense in the context of our relationship as writing teacher and student. An important role I played in the workshop was helping children identify meaningful topics. In this case, I had already identified James as someone who might need some help. In fact, I was anxious to help since I anticipated problems with James in the classroom if he went long without something to write about. In other words, I embraced two important teacher roles in my conversation with James. One was helping him find something to write about. The other was keeping order in the classroom, an order I thought might be upset if James did not find something to engage him.

I do not know what sort of weight James ascribed to my suggestion that he write a story about a fake line leader. When he talked about it at the end of the year, he said that I told him "maybe" he could write about that. James did not, by the end of the year, believe he was required to follow such suggestions from his writing teacher—he took me more or less at my word that he had a large amount of control over what and how he wrote (discussed later in chapter). But at the beginning of the year, when student control over text was perhaps not an assumption James made, my "maybe" could have meant "should" to James. Even if James heard maybe, my power as a teacher to assign work to children was part of the origins of this story. I had told James the day before that he *would* be doing some writing in my classroom. Whatever the personal meaningfulness or interest he found in such a story, James had the problem, by virtue of being a student in this writing workshop, of needing something to write about. In his interview, James noted that:

> In the beginning of the year when the writing workshop came we were like, yeah, it's going to be great, it's going to be great, we're going to have lots of time to write and stuff. But then when we really got there most, most of us we were like stumped on what to write about, and we couldn't figure out what to do.

James continued, asserting that children had a great deal of control over their work, but a basic requirement was that they write.

> Like, some of the people would go out in the hall and some people would go in the classroom. But Mr. Lensmire, he doesn't care where they are, what, and who they're working with, and if they're working with anybody, he just wants them to write. (Interview, 5-24-90)

My suggestion, therefore, provided a possible response by James to the problem of identifying and writing about something he chose, a problem he had not solved the day before. Thus, James found an idea for a story in a conversation with Kurt and me. The idea for his story depended on a school practice (lining up children) and emerged in anticipation of a school class—writing workshop. The conversation James participated in, as well as the story he eventually wrote with Ken, were shaped by me, a teacher who wanted to help James find something to write about, and who used his authority to keep order and require children to write in his classroom.

Besides my early influence on the story, the text of *The Fake Line Leader from Alabama* was also influenced by Grace, the regular classroom teacher. As I noted above, I had seen Grace talking with James and Ken (as well as writing on their paper) on the same day that these young authors allowed me to read their "going to bed" line. As you may have noticed, this line does not appear in their story. Grace replaced the line that would have read, "So they went to bed," with "So they had dinner together, sushi with hot fudge sauce." This line was written by Grace on the rough draft, and James confirmed, in his interview, that "sushi with hot fudge sauce" was Mrs. Parker's idea.

From an examination of the rough draft, it is clear that James and Ken had not written as far as the second reference to sushi before

Grace's intervention. Thus, Grace's intervention influenced the future development of their text. Minimally, it removed the event of Kurt and Lisa going to bed, replaced it with a dinner entre, and provided a phrase—sushi with hot fudge sauce—that is repeated three more times in the story. It is possible that her intervention also influenced the plot of the story: that Ken and James included "eating events"—lunch at school and lunch and dinner on the train—in order to use Grace's unusual suggestion. I am particularly interested in how Grace's intervention seemed to have shaped the ending of the story, which I interpret as a subtle resistance to the content and function of Grace's intervention.

I assume that Grace intervened where and how she did because of the sexual connotations of a line such as, "they went to bed." She intervened at no other point in their text. Ken and James themselves had identified this very line as a risky one when they wondered aloud whether or not to let me read it. The ending of their story is interesting, then, exactly because it reintroduces the sort of sexual connotations Grace had sought to remove.

When Lisa and Kurt finish their third meal of sushi and hot fudge sauce, they admit that they do not really like it. This makes sense, I suppose, and we might leave it at that. But after Kurt and Lisa get to Alabama, Lisa did two things: She rejected (again) sushi with hot fudge sauce with her, "I will cook you something *good*," and she invited Kurt to her house. The authors seem to be resisting or undoing Grace's intervention here—or at least, reasserting their own intention that a romantic relationship exists between Kurt and Lisa. The first time around, in the rough draft, dinner led to bed for the characters James and Ken created on the page. This is exactly the place Grace intervened. She frustrated Kurt and Lisa's desire—and James and Ken's desire to represent it on the page—but not for long. And remember that in the oral reading and interpretation of this story by James and Ken, they cemented the intimate relationship between Kurt and Lisa by saying that Kurt liked Lisa, and that the two eventually married.

James and Ken's appropriation of "sushi with hot fudge sauce" is a perfect example of how Bakhtin (1981) conceived of language learning and use. Originally, as I discussed in chapter 1, all words are someone else's words. Gradually, we take them over for our own purposes, but these words are "dialogic," they retain the intonations and evaluations of others even as they are used by us in new situations and transformed. In this case, "sushi with hot fudge sauce" were Grace's words, and used for the purpose of erasing a sexual relationship between Kurt and Lisa. Grace's words were heard in *The Fake Line Leader*, and they influenced James and Ken's story. But by the end of the story,

James and Ken seem to have largely appropriated Grace's words to their own ends. With Lisa and Kurt's rejection of sushi with hot fudge sauce at the end of the story, James and Ken created a space for the sort of romantic dinner and evening that Grace had sought to prohibit with her words.

Whether or not James and Ken were resisting Grace's intervention is less important for interpreting their text than the presence of romantic meanings in the story. Parts of James and Ken's text, and the sharing of their text, drew on common forms of teasing to elicit response from the class—a form of teasing that depends on typical gender arrangements among children in schools, in which "girls and boys are together, but mostly apart" (Thorne, 1986).

Heterosexual meanings could have found their way into James and Ken's text for a number of reasons. One reason might be that James and Ken wanted to test teacher boundaries of permissible content in their stories. Their bed line went over the line for Grace, as they assumed it might with me. Heterosexual meanings, then, might function like James' first choice of a writing topic (vomit) did—to challenge teacher and school norms of appropriate topics for talk and writing.

A second reason for the presence of heterosexual meanings might be the perceived demands of genre. Ken and James, in their readings and viewings of spy and secret agent stories, TV shows, and movies, might have acquired a sense that the male lead needs a love interest. So, Kurt, on the way to Michigan, meets Lisa. (In something of a reversal of stereotyped moves by men and women, Lisa initiated contact and later took the lead in getting Kurt to her house. Of course, the way to Kurt's heart was through his stomach.)

But another genre—often an oral one particular to children—might be more important. Thorne (1986) notes that, although Western culture tends to define children as relatively asexual, heterosexual language is sometimes used by adults and children to describe cross-sexual relationships. Furthermore:

> In everyday life in schools, heterosexual and romantic meanings infuse some ritualized forms of interactions between groups of boys and girls (e.g., "chase and kiss") and help maintain sex segregation. "Jimmy likes Beth" or "Beth likes Jimmy" is a major form of teasing, which a child risks in choosing to sit by or walk with someone of the other sex. (p. 177)

Girls and boys did not work together in the writing workshop when given the choice. In interviews, girls said they worked with other girls, boys with boys. I have only one example of a girl and boy working together, by choice, in my fieldnotes and the interviews. Suzanne and Rajesh collaborated for a short time in writing a story. Otherwise, all peer conferences and collaborations, as far as I can remember or tell from my data, had children working with other children of the same sex.

Thorne (1986) collected her data on playgrounds, in cafeterias, and in classrooms, and was especially interested in gender arrangements and their maintenance. She found that certain interactions between girls and boys seemed to lessen sex segregation, but that "gender-defined groups also come together in ways which emphasize their boundaries" (p. 172). The form of teasing mentioned above—"Beth likes Jimmy"—was one of the types of interaction that emphasized and maintained gender boundaries.

Children reported in their interviews that students in the workshop sometimes engaged in similar types of teasing *in their writing*. For example, Ken reported that someone (he did not say who) had written a story in which a child in the class, Bruce, "had a Barbie doll and he sleeps with it" (Interview, 5-31-90). The story achieved its provocativeness for young boys both from the sexual connotations of sleeping with a female, and from the suggestion that a boy would have a doll. And not just any doll, not a GI Joe, for example, but a Barbie doll. The story made fun of Bruce by suggesting a romantic relationship between him and a "girl" (Barbie doll), and by suggesting that he possessed a doll and played with it. In other words, Bruce "associated" with girls in the story—something these third grade boys avoided in the classroom—by having a relationship with one, and by doing something that has been traditionally labeled as a girl's activity (playing with dolls).

Carol and Sharon (named with Suzanne as one of the children illustrated in *The Fake Line Leader*) provided another example. They said that one way to tease a classmate was to name him or her in a story, and then to link the person to someone of the other sex.

SHARON: He used my name.
CAROL: And my name.
INTR: Really? Who did?
SHARON: Well, it was Bruce, Troy, and Ken, they used our name.
INTR: For what?
SHARON: They used girls' names that, that liked other boys.
INTR: Oh, and if—
CAROL: I think they used me with David, I'm not sure.
SHARON: They used me with um, Ken.
INTR: How do you feel about that?
SHARON: I didn't like it.
INTR: Why?

SHARON: Because you don't like somebody to use your name.
INTR: What, what can we do about that to change that?
SHARON: I told them not to write it and I told them, and they, they kept
     on writing and then I told Mrs. Parker and they erased my name out
     of it. Then they would write the story, they kept on saying that, um,
     that somebody in the story liked another person. (Interview, 5-30-90)

Stories that included characters named for children in the classroom,
and that suggested or stated romantic relationships among particular
boys and girls, were a problem for the children involved. Sharon and
Carol considered this a form of teasing. Sharon took action to make sure
she was not implicated in such teasing, but it seemed, if I interpret her
last comment correctly, with little success. Apparently, even if the written
record was changed, such teasing could then be sustained orally, with
utterances such as, "this character really stands for Sharon, even if the
name is different."

There are several aspects of the text and sharing of *The Fake Line
Leader* that suggest James and Ken's text participated in and responded
to the gender arrangements of children in this classroom, and oral and
written forms of teasing arising within these arrangements. First, characters in the story had the same names as children in the class. In fact, the
school and classroom Kurt visited is explicitly linked to Grace's classroom. And as I noted above, a romantic relationship was strongly suggested in the story—Lisa used a common opening line: "Is this seat
taken?"—and then she and Kurt had dinner together. They later ate lunch
and dinner again, and Lisa invited Kurt to her house.

Second, there was James' response to Suzanne's question as to why
Kurt revealed his name to Lisa. I was actually the first to respond to
Suzanne's question: "That's one of the jokes, right?" I said this because
James and I had talked about this aspect of the text before. While typing
the story for him and Ken, I noticed the inconsistency Suzanne later
noticed. When I asked James about this, he seemed alarmed—it was
clear that this was not an intentional aspect of the story. I suggested he
just leave it, because the inconsistency contributed to the humor of Kurt,
who seemed generally incompetent, and to stumble about and have
things happen to him. I was surprised, then, when I transcribed the
audiotape of this sharing session, to see how James explained Kurt's
lapse to Suzanne (I missed this shift as a participant in the classroom.)
James repeated my comment, and then said that Kurt forgot because of
his infatuation with Lisa. Ken affirmed the romantic relationship between
Kurt and Lisa by extending the story even further into the future than I
had above—in the end, Ken said, they got married.

I am not saying that the only intention or purpose Ken and James had for writing their story was to tease Kurt and Lisa, or that it even was necessarily one of their intentions. Kurt's inclusion in the story, especially, could have been largely accidental—the product of being at the head of the line with James and me. Still, Kurt was not a member of James' close group of friends, and, as will become evident later in the chapter, James and his friends were not always on the best of terms with girls in the class. There may have been some conflict between Lisa and the authors I do not know about that encouraged James and Ken to single Lisa out and include her in the story. Or, she may have been included because she, with Suzanne, was one of the most popular girls in the class. (And remember, Suzanne was also included in the story, when James and Ken said that she and Sharon were in one of their illustrations.)

Also, I am not saying that gender divisions and romantic meanings exhaust what James and Ken were doing in their story and their sharing of it. I have already discussed Grace and my interventions into their work, and the authors' responses to those influences. In addition, James and Ken evaluate, negatively it seems, "hippies" and their hairstyles. And during sharing time, James poked fun at one of Ken's drawings, and James and Ken got a laugh by connecting two girls in the class with more or less well-executed (supposed) drawings of them in the book. (Of course, this may very well have been teasing across the gender divide—two boys scoring off two girls by making them "look silly.")

I *am* arguing that James and Ken, in their attempt to create a funny, entertaining text, drew on heterosexual meanings to provoke response, both from teachers and students. Even if Kurt and Lisa were not specific targets of teasing, the story drew on the suggestion of a romantic relationship among real, third grade children for effect. James and Ken were writing in a social context in which teachers suppressed references to sex, and boys and girls separated themselves from each other in their work in peer conferences and collaborations. Children avoided situations (and worked to change texts) that might suggest they liked someone of the other sex. In such a context, this story—with its real children and romantic liaisons—could stir things up, bringing laughter, more teasing, denials, and speculation. And Ken and James seemed to know what they were doing, to know what would provoke response, especially as they shared their text.

At the time, I did not know what they were doing, did not understand much about the sorts of cultural resources they were drawing on, and the possible consequences for other children of their story. If I had, instead of recording descriptions of this sharing time such as "children were laughing," and noting that "things went well" (Fieldnotes, 11-28-89), I might have noticed that certain children were laughing, and others were not.

I have shown some of the ways that James and Ken's work on *The Fake Line Leader* was affected by the social context within which they were writing and sharing. I have looked to the social origins of the story, teacher interventions, and a gendered, divided student culture to make sense of aspects of their written and oral texts. But we must be careful not to let considerations of social context overdetermine our conceptions of who James and Ken were in the workshop, and what they were about.

In what follows, I explore some of the ways in which James and his friends asserted themselves in the writing workshop, examine some of the intentions they pursued, and some of the consequences of their actions. I look to their relations with each other, with other children in the room, and with teachers. In these discussions, I focus on James, for at least three reasons. First, his responses in his interview were often quite revealing. Second, and more importantly, James was a prominent figure in the student culture, and especially within the small group of boys—including Ken, Bruce, Troy, and Paul—he worked and played with in the workshop, and in and out of school. He represented the values of this group of boys well, and, through him, a sense of the workings of student intention and peer relations, and their influences on children's writing, can begin to be developed (chapters 4 and 5 extend this discussion).

Finally, the story of *The Fake Line Leader* is not over yet, neither for James nor for me. James made it into something like his life work in the workshop. With Ken, he wrote a long sequel to their first text—*Part 2*—and then with Paul, Troy, and/or possibly Ken and/or Bruce, he wrote *Part 3* (on the rough draft of the third installment, Bruce was listed as one of the authors, and his name was written over Ken's name, which had been erased). James wrote other pieces, but nothing with the sustained attention and detail that characterized the *Line Leader* trilogy. I attempt to make sense of James sticking with these stories, and argue that the series of stories became one of the ways that James and his friends asserted their positions at the top of the peer hierarchy in the classroom. Eventually, they took the story of *The Fake Line Leader from Alabama* away from Kurt and Lisa, and put themselves at the focus of the fictional worlds they created.

———

INTR: Tell me James, who are the popular kids in class?
JAMES: Um. Popular kids in the class. I wouldn't know. I would probably be one of the more popular kids in the class, but—

INTR: Why are you popular?

JAMES: I don't know why I'm popular. Because of. . . . And Suzanne is
    one of the popular girls. Robert is pretty popular, but not as me. I'm
    probably the most popular boy in the class, probably.

INTR: Why do you think you're more popular than Robert?

JAMES: Robert? Well, because Robert tries to be funny when he isn't funny.

INTR: And you?

JAMES: Well, I basically am funny. Most of the time I am funny.

INTR: Funny about what things?

JAMES: Well, it depends what kind of things are happening. I can make
    like most serious things funny.

INTR: People like that in class?

JAMES: Some people do.

INTR: Why are you funny?

JAMES: I don't know why I'm funny, I get, sometimes I'm in the mood to be
    funny, so I get funny, I just say OK, I'm going to be funny now, so.

INTR: What are the times that you feel in the mood to be funny?

JAMES: The times, when the day's kind of going slow, and it's really not
    going, nobody's really having any fun. (Interview, 5-24-90; unless
    noted, quotations from James that follow are from this interview)

James characterized himself as funny. In fact, he seemed to link his
popularity to being funny: He was more popular than Robert, who was
"pretty popular," because Robert tried to be funny (but failed), whereas
James really was funny. His performance in the sharing of *The Fake Line
Leader* showed his ability to make other children in the class laugh. His
performances were not limited to sharing time, however, or to the writing workshop. James hinted at the sorts of school situations he liked to
be funny in above—he liked to "make serious things funny," "when the
day's kind of going slow," when "nobody's really having any fun." At
least one sense of being "funny" for James, then, was responding specifically to school and its boredom or demands. Or, put another way, being
funny was one of the ways James resisted teacher and school attempts to
control him.

James was one of three children I took to the principal's office during the school year, exactly because he was funny. One such time was
when Grace stayed home sick. I had watched the substitute teacher
struggling to conduct his lessons because of children's behavior. Many
children were involved, including Troy and Bruce, who tried several
times to get "the wave" started from their positions at the corner of the
large halfsquare of desks that formed the outer boundary of student
desks that day—they became quite angry with Lisa, the next person in

line, when she did not follow their lead and throw her hands into the air at the appropriate time. But James was prominent in the substitute teacher's struggle. When it was time for the writing workshop to begin, the substitute teacher left the room to talk to the principal.

> I told the class that I had been watching what they were doing, and that I was ashamed of them and angry. I told them that they had been running the substitute teacher around like (and I stumbled here for words) one of those moving targets at a carnival booth, where, in cartoons, the target is a person or animal who moves one way until it gets hit, and then goes the other way, and on and on. I had their attention. There was silence, then James, with enthusiasm: "Yeah, that would be neat." I gave him a warning, and continued my sermon, but some of the children were smiling. (Fieldnotes, 11-30-89)

James did not get sent to the principal's office for his comment—that happened a little later when he wore me down with continued commentary. James also wore down Grace a few times, and from what I heard around school, the music teacher and the art teacher. At least some of these troubles were linked, I am sure, to times when James said to himself, "OK, I'm going to be funny now," and was a little too effective.

James also thought of himself as quite popular, and this self-characterization matches well with what other children in the room said about him and my own sense of who he was among peers. In the interviews, most children identified him as one of the popular boys, if not the most popular (I should note that some children made a distinction, saying that James was popular, but not with *them*). In various fieldnotes across the year and for various reasons, I wrote of James as having a "high status among the children," being part of the "in-group," that he was "cool," "powerful." In his interview, Rajesh identified James as the leader of a secret club whose members made up the group of boys with whom James worked in the workshop.

INTR: Who are the popular kids in the class?
RAJESH: James, Bruce, Paul, and Ken.
INTR: Why do you think people are, why do you think—
RAJESH Well, James, James, I'll tell you about the boys. I know a lot about the boys and I know how they got famous too.
INTR: How do they get famous?
RAJESH Because of that stupid club. They belong to a secret club. (Interview, 5-18-90)

Rajesh apparently got his information first hand. According to him, James and his friends asked him to be in their club at the beginning of the year, but later rejected him. James was the leader of that group, and he and Ken formed the core of the club, with Paul, Troy, and Bruce becoming more closely associated with them as the year progressed, at least in the workshop. Bruce was tied to the group primarily (it seemed from his interview) through his close friendship with Troy. He said he also liked to work with Ken, Paul, and sometimes Rajesh, but not with James—Bruce said he could not trust James with secrets about his stories, and that James did not tell him that his stories were good, as Paul and Luke did. Rajesh reported being a part of the group early in the year. My fieldnotes have him writing collaboratively with Troy and Bruce in early December. After the winter holidays, he worked with Kurt, who was not part of the club.

James and his friends conferenced almost exclusively with each other in the writing workshop: Rajesh even claimed in his interview that James demanded such exclusivity from members of the club. The primary reason James and the others gave for working with each other was friendship. Often, these friendships were described in terms of relationships that were developed and maintained outside of the writing workshop, and that involved trust. Bruce, for example, said, "Troy I trust the most because he's been my friend for a long time, since preschool. Actually longer than that" (Interview, 5-21-90). James, Ken, and Troy played on the same local youth soccer team, and James noted that as one reason he liked to work with them in the workshop. James also said that "Troy likes most of the same things that I like," and that he liked to work with Paul, "because he does a lot of sports and we can talk about stuff like sports."

James valued the chance to talk with his friends in peer conferences and collaborations, and valued the advice and opinions his peers shared there. In fact, from what he said in his interview, it appeared that what peers said to him about his texts was just as important as, if not more important than, what I said to him in teacher-student writing conferences. James discussed his use of teacher suggestions:

INTR: If he [Mr. Lensmire] gave you advice or a suggestion on how to make things better, did you always follow the advice?

JAMES: Not always, because sometimes I would, he said, you don't have to do this but, all the time he says, you don't have to do this but I think it would be better. And I felt the other way would be better so I didn't do what he told me.

INTR: But aren't you supposed to listen to a teacher?

JAMES: Yes, yes, I am, but, um, most of the time, if the teacher says something, yet I don't think it's the right thing to do, so I don't do it.

INTR: Right. Why isn't it the right thing to do?

JAMES: Because sometimes, like one time he said I think you should change this in the story, but really when I kept that people really liked that part of it.

As a teacher in writing conferences, I was worried about dominating student ideas and intentions because of my institutional authority. James related one of the ways that I displayed this worry in conferences—I told him he did not have to do what I said, but that this or that might be helpful. James tested my suggestions against his own sense of what would work best. In his last comment above, however, he referred to his peers, and justified not using my suggestion, in part, by saying that his peers really liked what he did not change.

With teacher suggestions, James talked about deciding for himself whether or not to use them. He talked quite differently about how he dealt with peer comments.

JAMES: The conferences with classmates. Um. I would ask them questions say, should I keep this, do you like this, what don't you like so I could take it out. But I didn't really take it out until like two people said it wasn't good.
INTR: Why two people?
JAMES: Because you know one person might be like, you know, not like it, but another person might really like it.
INTR: So then what would you do, if one did and one didn't. How would you make this decision?
JAMES: I would ask another person.

I do not know if James actually followed such a procedure in his writing process. That is not as important for my purposes as the weight James appeared to give his peers' suggestions. James seemed much more comfortable ignoring my suggestions than he did his peers' suggestions. Even if he did not go from boy to boy within his group of friends, checking off who did and did not like something, it is clear he attached great significance to their opinions.

One of the things this group of boys valued were entertaining stories. In response to a question about what kinds of writing he liked to do, James replied, "I like to write the comedy stuff like, like one of my books was the Fake Line Leader from Alabama. . . . It was a funny book because he said they were eating sushi with hot fudge sauce, and he was a line leader, but he was a spy really and a fake." Ken reported he liked to write funny stories as well. Paul said he wrote fantasy; Bruce, action stories.

The titles of some of their stories suggest this demand for entertaining, exciting, sometimes humorous texts: *The Magic Triceratops*, by Troy; *Me and My Dinosaur* and *Back to the Future, Part IV*, by Ken; *The Crabs Meet Friends* by Bruce, Troy, and Ken. Some of these and other texts written by James and his friends included, in fictional narratives, the names of children from the class (and sometimes adults from the school). We saw this in James and Ken's *The Fake Line Leader*. Ken wrote one story called, *All About Ken, Troy, and James*; and collaborated with Bruce and Troy on *Crabs*, which featured the three authors as crabs in the ocean. Early in the year, Rajesh wrote a story in which Clifford's gym teacher was actually an alien from outer space. Rajesh's final line was: "And so I, Rajesh, stabbed him in the heart." (This was the final line of the revised version. Rajesh's original version had no ending. I talked with Rajesh about his story in several writing conferences, and he said that his story-without-an-ending was exactly the way he wanted it. Then he took it home for his mother to type. Parents, sometimes, are powerful contextual influences on the narratives of children.)

I have been characterizing James and his friends' work in the classroom in terms of what/who they included and valued. They were a small group of friends who worked together in conferences and collaborations on stories. They wrote and enjoyed funny, entertaining fictional texts that sometimes included children from the classroom as characters.

But as Solloro (1990), writing on ethnicity, notes, groups are defined not so much as things-in-themselves, but in relation to other groups, by way of contrast. In other words, a significant aspect of a groups' identity rests in its exclusions, by its members doing or being *not this*. In what follows, I sketch some of the exclusions this group of boys made in their work with peers. I focus on James, again, as an articulate member of this group and its leader. Then, I conclude the chapter with an examination of the sequels to *The Fake Line Leader from Alabama*, especially *Part 2*, and show how these texts draw on social relations among children in this workshop for their meaning.

I have already suggested, in my discussion of the group's composition and boundaries, some of the most obvious exclusions James and his friends made in their day-to-day work in the writing workshop. James did not work with most of the boys in the class, or with any of the girls.

INTR: Is there anyone you really don't ever want to conference with?
JAMES: Yeah, most of the girls.

INTR: Most of the girls? Why?
JAMES: I don't know. I just. . . . Because I think they, they'll have. I don't
   know.

   James would not elaborate here, but later suggested a reason he did
not want to conference with girls when he talked about sharing his texts
in front of the class.

   Most of the girls I don't want to read in front of because they have
   probably different opinions and they don't, some of the, most of
   them probably don't like me. I mean I don't care what they say, I like
   my piece.

   James seemed to expect conflict with girls—they would have different opinions and they would not like him or his work. In their interviews, a number of girls, though not all, *did* single out James as someone they particularly disliked. Often, they reported that James teased
girls, in and out of the workshop.
   Besides gender, social class seemed something of a boundary for James
and his friends. Among male classmates, James named four boys with
whom he especially did not want to work. Of these four, three were from
the trailer court—Robert, Bartleby, and Leon. The fourth, John, was often
unable to deal with his frustration and anger with teachers and classmates.
He cried often, and, on occasion, bit classmates who seemed to enjoy pro-
voking him. John also happened to be one of the most talented writers in
the room.

INTR: Why wouldn't you like to work with them?
JAMES: Um. They just, sometimes, you know how John, you've seen John
   and um, and Leon is just, he tries to do stuff that he really can't do,
   and he tries to do more than he is.
INTR: Why does that bother you?
JAMES: Because I mean, I like people because they be themselves, and I
   don't care how they, if they try. If they try and act what they aren't
   then I don't like them because they are just not the person that they
   really are.

   From his privileged position in the social hierarchy of boys in the
room, James identified four children much lower in that hierarchy who
were undesirable to work with as peer collaborators and audiences.
James had opposed himself to Robert earlier in the interview, because
Robert tried to be funny, but was not, according to James. James had

linked his own popularity to being funny, and Robert seemed to represent some sort of competition for him. Here, James suggests that Leon was acting in ways inappropriate for his location in the peer hierarchy. James specified the problem with Leon a little later in the interview.

> He [Leon] tries to be real, someone he isn't, and really that is he tries to be, tries to be really cool and stuff, you know, and he's not.

Obviously, social class was not the only thing at work in excluding boys from James' group—many of the boys excluded were also from middle class backgrounds. But it was important. James' comments suggest various distances among groups of boys, or different permeabilities of boundaries. Someone like David, for example, who played soccer with James and Ken, and lived in their neighborhood, crossed the group's boundaries on occasion to work with Bruce and Paul in conferences. This did not happen with children from the trailer park, with Robert and Leon—that boundary seemed harder to cross.

Before I move to James and his friends' texts, I want to make one final point about the exclusions James and his friends made in their day-to-day work in the writing workshop: Other children felt them. James and his friends acted out these exclusions, acted out their evaluations of other children in the room—they did not just express them in interviews. Thus, Robert complained about James and Troy bragging that their clothes were better than his: "They think their clothes is one of the best things in the world" (Interview, 5-24-90); Sharon talked about James and his friends giving her "bad feelings. . . . They laugh at your stories, because they just think they're more powerful and they have better stories and stuff like that" (Interview, 5-30-90); and Rajesh came to me at the round table one day, careful to keep his back to the rest of the class:

> Rajesh told me he had something "very important" to talk about with me. He said the words with feeling, and his voice broke several times. It didn't seem easy for him to talk to me about what he wanted to tell me.
>
> I like Rajesh a lot. He was one of the first kids I really started liking in the class. He was the first one to play with my long hair and tell me I should put it in a pony tail. He used to come over by me and sit on my leg while I talked to someone else at the table. So seeing Rajesh hurting hurt me too. But there was also a strategic, serious aspect to his words and tone. It seemed he felt he needed to persuade me of what he was saying.
>
> What he was saying was that James was trying to get Paul to "turn away" from Rajesh, to not be Rajesh's friend anymore. He said that he didn't have many friends, and now James was trying to turn Paul away

from him. Paul had been collaborating with him, but now Paul was working with James. And he didn't think that Paul would ever conference with him now, even if he asked him. This seemed to be the thing that upset Rajesh the most, that Paul wouldn't conference with him if he asked him to (another risky moment in the safe writing workshop). (Fieldnotes, 2-23-90)

In this case, I was able to help Rajesh a little, by talking to Paul with Rajesh at my side. Paul said he would conference with Rajesh if Rajesh wanted him to. But of course, children lead lives outside of the classroom, and if more direct action than whispered words behind the teacher's back is needed, there is always the playground.

SHARON: Outside today James was, James and Bruce were pushing Rajesh.
INTR: Why?
SHARON: Because he's an Indian.
INTR: What's it? I don't understand.
SHARON: Neither do—
CAROL: He's just an Indian.
SHARON: They want to have a reason.
CAROL: They tease Rajesh because Rajesh believes in different gods.
INTR: Really?
CAROL: I think that's part of the reasons, stuff like that.
INTR: Uh huh. And um, any other reasons?
CAROL: They think he's a wimp so they—
SHARON: Push him.
CAROL: Yeah.
INTR: And what does Rajesh do?
SHARON: Just stands there, let them push him.
INTR: Does he have any friends?
CAROL: Yeah I think he has a couple. (Interview, 5-30-90)

The interview segment is, of course, somewhat unfair to James, Bruce, and Rajesh, and depends on the careful lifting of this and not that from the transcript. Other children were teased (our informants mentioned Jil, Jessie, and John), and other people besides James and Bruce picked on Rajesh.

These bits of editing cast James and Bruce as third grade bigots and Rajesh as a passive victim. Quick, simple accusations of racial and ethnic/religious intolerance, however, should not be made against James and Bruce. One of James and Bruce's best friends—Ken—was black. And Rajesh had once been a part of their group. In the end, it was Sharon and Carol who attributed racial or ethnic motivations to James and Bruce's actions. This does not mean that they were not correct, or at least partly correct in their assessment of the situation. But whatever the reasons Rajesh got pushed around, he got pushed around. And his struggles to make and keep friends, his struggles to find classmates with whom to conference and collaborate—these struggles were caught up with James' status and influence among peers, and affected Rajesh's experiences in the workshop.

———

James and his friends also "acted out" their relations to and evaluations of other children in the room in their texts. Above, I argued that gender arrangements of girls and boys in this classroom were important for understanding the meanings of James and Ken's first *Line Leader* story. In their future work, they continued to draw on this aspect of the student culture, but it became less prominent. In Parts 2 and 3 of James' *Line Leader* trilogy, status differences among children in the room take on much greater importance for interpreting what is happening in their fiction. These stories were a place for James and his friends to comment on social relations in the classroom. Given their position at the top of the informal pecking order, it was fitting that they soon wrote themselves into their stories as the main characters, and placed themselves at the center of attention of the fictional worlds they created.

One of Ken's stories, *All About Ken, Troy, and James*, will serve as an excellent introduction to the later *Line Leader* stories, because it was much less subtle than those texts often were. Ken's story set up a hierarchy of characters based on size and strength. The title and the action of the story affirmed the solidarity of Ken, Troy, and James, who were dinosaurs in the story. They confronted, in the first scene, three other (smaller) dinosaurs who had the names of three other boys in the class:

> Me and Troy and James were running after three Pterodactyl. Their names are Robert and William and Bruce, and Robert and William and Bruce flew down. And then James ran up to get William and Troy ran up to get Robert. And Ken went up to get Bruce. And James said, "Look who I caught, a little squirt."

Robert and William were from the trailer park, and Robert was singled out by James, remember, as someone with whom he did not want to work. Bruce was a somewhat ambivalent member of James' group, especially at the beginning of the year—very good friends with Troy, but not so good with James. It may be that nothing insulting was intended by Ken with his text. In fact, there may be some status attached to being included in one of Ken's stories. I had asked Ken once during the year

to work with William on a story William was revising, and he had agreed
to do it with no visible resistance. Still, the story pits three friends—Ken,
Troy, and James, with superior size and strength as dinosaurs—against
three other classmates—Robert, William, and Bruce—with lower status in
the room. William is called a "little squirt" (he was one of the smallest
boys in the class). Whatever Ken's intent or the positive significance of
being included in one of Ken's texts, his story reproduced, in text, social
relations among boys in the classroom.

James and Ken's sequel to their first *Line Leader* story also participated in and commented on social relations in the room, but was less
straightforward. All the characters in the story were named for children
in the class. There was no mention of Robert as Kurt's boss this time: The
character was referred to only as "his boss." There was a residual connection between Kurt and Lisa, but romantic aspects of their relationship
were not emphasized. In fact, the first page and a half (of four handwrit-
ten pages in their rough draft) seemed less a story and more a vehicle for
mentioning popular children's names. Kurt got a phone call from his
boss, and was told to report to Clifford again (there was no specific reason or task given for going there). You are not missing the plot in the
two excerpts below—the only action in nearly the first half of the story
was the introduction of different people to each other:

> Soon he [Kurt] was at school. He found Mrs. P's class and found Lisa.
> Lisa said, "Meet some of my friends, like Sharon, one of my best
> friends."
> "Hi Sharon, nice to meet you."
> "Nice to meet you Kurt. Oh Lisa, there is Suzanne."
> "Oh yes, how could I forget Suzanne, one of my best friends."

And a little later:

> Kurt was walking alone and saw Troy. "Hello, my name is Kurt. What
> is your name?"
> "My name is Troy. Nice to meet you."
> "Nice to meet you too."
> "I am sort of a bully."
> "Oh you shouldn't be."
> "O.K. I won't be. I like you, you're sort of funny."

I do not know enough about the details of friendships in the room
at the time this was written to understand what a text like this might
mean to Lisa, Sharon, and Suzanne. All three of the girls were quite popular, but I have no record of them working together with each other in
the workshop. It is possible that Ken and James knew they were *not*

friends, and hoped to provoke response by making them best friends in the story. (It is also possible that these girls would simply object to being in the story in the first place, perhaps because they viewed it as a type of association with boys that they were trying to avoid. Eventually, a rule emerged in the workshop that required authors, before sharing or publishing their stories, to get the permission of children whose names appeared in their stories. I discuss this rule and the issues surrounding the use of classmates' names in stories in chapter 6.)

It is also interesting to speculate about Troy's inclusion above. When James and Ken started writing this text (early October), Troy had not yet begun collaborating with them in the workshop. He had written alone and with Bruce and Rajesh. This text could represent something of a bid for him to be their friend: Don't be a bully, be our friend.

In a slightly revised version of this story that I photocopied in February (the above was typed from a rough draft from November), Troy's name had been erased throughout the text of *Part 2*, and David's name put in its place. By this time, Troy was actively collaborating with James and Paul on the third part of the trilogy. I do not know who changed the name from Troy to David in the first sequel, or why it was changed, but a few scenes involving David/Troy a little later in the story might provide a clue.

At the end of the school day spent introducing (popular) children to each other, Kurt, Lisa, and David/Troy boarded a plane for Hawaii (that they thought was going to Tennessee). On the plane, David/Troy met Carol, and started talking to her. Eventually, they and Kurt and Lisa went to Carol's house.

> [David/Troy] "What makes you go so far from home?"
> [Carol] "Oh, I'm going back to Hawaii."
> "You mean this is the plane to Hawaii and not Tennessee?"
> "Yes!"
> "Oh! Can we come to your house?"
> "What do you mean, 'we'?"
> "Oh, I mean Kurt and Lisa."
> "Oh, I like Kurt and Lisa."
> "Well don't you like me?"
> "Yes, I love you!"
> They landed in Hawaii and got off. They went to Carol's house. When they got to Carol's house she opened the door. The house was pretty.
> Kurt said, "Who was your decorator? Are you rich Carol?"
> Carol said, "No, er, yes. Would you like to come in my bedroom?"
> "No way!"
> "Just kidding, just kidding."
> "Whoa!"

My guess is that when Troy started working with James and Paul on *Part 3*, he had access to *Part 2*, and that he objected to the sort of romantic relationship suggested between him and Carol by "I love you," and the bedroom talk that followed. The bedroom talk was interesting, and its meaning(s) not at all· clear. Carol seemed thrown off-guard, or at least made uncomfortable, by Kurt's question as to whether or not she was rich. She eventually admitted she was, and then asked someone or all of them if he/she/they would like to come into her bedroom. Her question could be interpreted as a continuation of showing the house to the guests: this is the living room, and would you like to see my bedroom? Kurt, or David/Troy, or Lisa answer quite vehemently, "No way!" responding to the possible sexual connotations of the question. James and Ken seem to have been playing with double meanings and the embarrassment or humor that could result. In any event, this and the earlier scene suggested a romantic connection between David/Troy and Carol. (They also associated Carol with a fine house and money.) David may have seemed an appropriate replacement for Troy in the story—he was not unpopular, but he was also not immediately involved with James, Paul, Ken, and Troy when they were writing and rewriting their *Line Leader* stories.

A strange thing happened next in James and Ken's story. Our main characters went to a Taco Bell in Hawaii, where they found their teachers and almost all of their classmates from Clifford happily chomping on nachos. The authors listed all the children and teachers (Grace, Ruth, and me) who were there, and missed only two of the twenty-seven children in the room in their list—William and Bartleby. They wrote: "The whole class was there. Rajesh, Leon, Maya," and on and on. It is difficult to understand why James and Ken would list all these names in their story. If I were feeling generous, I might interpret their inclusion of all these children and teachers as a recognition, on their part, of other people's feelings—that they recognized that their classmates and teachers might feel left out if some and not others were included in stories told in the workshop. In chapter 5, I discuss a sharing session in which Lisa told her classmates that they should not worry if they did not appear in the story she was reading to them that day, because she had not finished yet, and she would eventually write everyone into it. I must note, however, that even if the authors were concerned that children and teachers not feel left out, there were two children left out of the story—and both children lived in the trailer park.

But I lean toward a different interpretation. I think that James and Ken needed all the children and the teachers at the Taco Bell so that their classmates and teachers were present to acknowledge the rightful place of James and his friends at the top of the classroom heap. Let me explain. When the main characters of the story thus far—Kurt, Lisa, Carol, and David—arrived at the Taco Bell, James and Ken listed themselves, as well as Troy and Paul, with the other children already there. This was the first time that James wrote himself as a character into one of his stories (Ken had already done this in *All About Ken, Troy, and James*, discussed above). Soon after Kurt and the others arrived, the characters of James, Ken, Troy, and Paul, left for the beach to do some surfing. They also took control of the story, became its main characters:

> Hours passed. Paul came running up to the Taco Bell. He was yelling."Ken, Troy, and James got caught by a humongous wave. They did a backwards flip in the air. And that's the best anyone has ever done before!"
> The whole class said, "Hey, how do you know?"
> Paul said, "I know. I own a surf shop."
> "Mr. Lensmire said I could write a story about this."
> "No way, I'm getting out of here." So James, Ken, Troy, Paul went. . .
>   TO BE CONTINUED

And the story was continued, in *Part 3*. There, James and his friends were the main characters from the start. They were the ones flying in airplanes (to Florida this time) and going to fast food restaurants (McDonald's). Kurt and Lisa were heard from briefly (it seemed it would not be a *Line Leader* story without them), but the story focused throughout on James, Ken, Troy, and Paul, with appearances from Bruce, at the beach, and Rajesh and David, at McDonald's.

But the important shift had occurred in *Part 2*. There, the boys left their classmates and teachers at the Taco Bell, and went to the beach. Paul came back with a story about them, and made the assertion, in front of everyone, that his friends had surfed better than anyone else ever had. This assertion was questioned by the whole class, but Paul answered, "*I know.*" James and his friends, in their fiction, asserted their place in the classroom. They were the best. Children in the room might question this, but James and his friends knew. They were the best.

Actually, James and Ken had not waited until the second *Line Leader* to proclaim this in print. After their first story had been typed and bound, they added an "About the Authors" section, printed in black magic marker, on a blank page at the end of the book. This is what James and Ken wrote:

> About the Authers
> their relly Hip
> nobody can be better
> than them dude
> their tubylr to the max!
> So their the best!!!

At the end of *Part 2*, James and Ken even got a little dig in at me and the writing workshop. An unidentified speaker reported that I had said, again, what I had said to James at the beginning of the year, and at the beginning of *The Fake Line Leader from Alabama*: You could write a story about this. Another unidentified speaker—I assume, with no evidence, that it was James—answered back, "No way. I'm getting out of here." James would rather be at the beach than in school, rather have experiences than write about them. (Of course, like other American Romantics who worshipped experience in the real world and condemned the bookish world of schools, James wrote this in a book. Then again, Thoreau and Twain were not third graders who had little choice as to whether or not they would write.)

———

The structure and norms of the workshop were explicitly developed to allow children to choose and pursue meaningful projects across the school year. James and his friends did this, and they brought meanings and values from the playground, the cafeteria, and their own histories, into the workshop. But it would be wrong to see James' project as "something which, having in some way taken shape and definition in the psyche of an individual, [was] outwardly objectified for others with the help of external signs of some kind" (Volosinov, 1973, p. 84). A Romantic conception of James and his friends' writing and its meanings is wholly inadequate. Their projects were determined both from within and without, and emerged within relations with classmates and teachers, in the clash and sharing of values and meanings, expressed in oral and written texts, in interactions.

James and his friends were powerful figures in the peer culture. Their actions were strongly defined by their efforts to exert control in their relations with other children and their teachers. A major theme of the writing they produced, especially James, was social relations—commenting on them, working them out, excluding and including certain children, resisting teacher authority to demand work and control their texts and lives in school. James and his friends enacted their projects from the top of a peer hierarchy of boys, and largely in opposition to the girls. Their projects were disturbing for their influences on other children and the boys themselves, for their inclusions and exclusions, for their nascent politics.

Chapter 4

Peer Audiences and Risk

I asked Karen if she would like to share her recently published book, *Mrs.P. and Her Lovebird:*

One day there was a little girl named Mrs. P. She thought of that name because she wanted to be a teacher. But her real name is Grace.
The thing that Grace liked: her dog. Her dog's name was Hooey. Every day she let him outside. And he would howl. And one day she let him out, he howled again. And the people that were next to her house, they called the police. And they took him away. And Grace was very sad.
    Something about her boyfriend. Grace was in the 5th grade. One day she met this boy. And he liked her a lot. And she liked him too. And then they got to 6th grade. And he became her boyfriend.

Karen has never shared her own work in front of the class—I even had to half drag her over to Jil once to get her to have a peer conference. Karen shook her head no. I enlisted the aid of Kurt and John, and told her they would like to hear her story. They immediately caught on and played their part, asked her to please read her story to them. I suggested we go out into the hall, possibly a less threatening place for Karen to read. Karen went to get her book from the library, and Kurt, John, Jessie, and I went into the hall.
    We all sat on the floor, in a sort of semicircle with Karen in front of us, with her back to the brick wall of the hallway. She was still hesitant, but with encouragement from me and the other children, she picked up her book and read her title. She was a little agitated, and occasionally rocked, with legs crossed, from her seated position almost up unto her knees, and back down again.
    As she started reading her story, Ken quietly joined our group. I remember being impressed with how Ken did it. He walked behind the semicircle, and sort of crawled in right beside me, on my right. I

71

briefly put my arm around him and gave him a little hug as he sat next to me. I was impressed because it was almost as if Ken knew that Karen was a reluctant sharer, and was trying to be as unintimidating and undisruptive as possible. I was very pleased with him.

Karen was not. She immediately stopped reading, rocked forward, and handed the book to me and said, "You read." (Karen immediately moved to a method she had used before to get her piece heard—she wanted someone else to read it, almost as if she didn't want to use her own voice—was it too close? too vulnerable? or was it facing an audience, being too present?—Janis had read Karen's first published piece earlier in the year.) I tried persuading Karen to continue reading, but she shook her head no. It was fairly clear that Ken was the reason she wouldn't read. While Ken was there, I couldn't get Karen to read. Ken seemed to know this. I didn't tell Ken to leave, but very quickly he did, and soon Karen was reading again. A little later Janis slid into the semicircle where Ken was, but Karen kept reading. She soon finished her book.

I was proud of how Karen's classmates responded to her text—they really seemed to try to make Karen feel good after she read. John picked up on what I thought was a wonderful problem at the beginning of the story—Karen is writing about Mrs. Parker as a little girl, and starts her story with, "One day there was a little girl named Mrs. P." Then, Karen tries to write her way out of a child being called Mrs. P: "She thought of that name because she wanted to be a teacher. But her real name is Grace." John doubted that Mrs. Parker, as a little girl, would call herself by her married name. I thought it was pretty impressive to pick this up in an oral reading. Karen didn't seem threatened, and she was soon telling us that she was going to write her next story about her baby bird dying.

I wanted to find out why Karen wouldn't read in front of Ken, so after the workshop was over, I asked Karen to go out in the hall with me again. I asked her why she wouldn't share with Ken there. At first she said, "Too many people." When I questioned this, saying that Janis had come out later, replacing Ken, and she still read, Karen said, "I don't know." I asked her if she had been worried that Ken wouldn't like her story, and she nodded her head yes. But I couldn't tell if she meant it or if I had just given her a way to satisfy me and she took it. She seemed nervous, so I stopped asking her questions and we went back into the classroom.

A little later, as I sat at my round table, Karen walked up to me, carrying a large sheet of construction paper, folded in half and stapled to form a sort of envelop/pocket. Karen often does stuff like this with paper, and has given me such pockets as gifts. On one side was written, "I'm sorry Ken." (Maybe she would give it to Ken.) As she showed it to me, she said, "Look what I wrote and I wasn't even looking."

I don't know what the "not looking" part meant, but I interpreted the "I'm sorry" as meaning that Karen had thought I had been reprimanding her in the hall before—that I was saying she had done something wrong to Ken by not reading in front of him.

I quickly told her I wasn't yelling at her, that I was "just wondering" about why she didn't want to share with Ken there. I tried to reassure her—I really hadn't been angry or disappointed in her—because her sharing in front of a few people and getting their response was a breakthrough for her, I thought. Karen was standing next to me, and I grabbed her shoulders and told her that she hadn't done anything wrong and that next time she wanted to share I would ask her who she would like to read to. She responded that she didn't like reading to the whole class, and that she was going to start a new story the next day. (Fieldnotes, 3-22-90)

I develop two themes in this chapter. One, rather dramatically represented in Karen's story, is the influence multiple audiences, more or less desirable and trusted by individual authors, exerted on the experiences and texts of children in this classroom. In the sharing session with Karen, I had selected Kurt, John, and Jessie as an audience for her story exactly because I had guessed they represented a fairly safe and comfortable group for her. Janis also seems to have been a trusted audience—Ken, apparently was not. When Ken joined the group, he effectively silenced Karen in the sharing of her text, despite what I perceived as his efforts to not disrupt her reading. One of the subtexts of my discussion of James and his friends was how their intentions and actions—constrained but also set free within the workshop setting—might make the classroom a less supportive or comfortable place for others to write. In what follows, I look especially (but not exclusively) to children on the other end of the peer hierarchy for their perceptions of peers as audiences for their work. The classroom seems a riskier place to write for some of these children than it did for popular, powerful children.

As a teacher, I had limited access to and influence over the workings of these multiple peer audiences. Above, I tried to find out why Karen did not want to read in front of Ken. I was quite interested in what Karen would say, both as a teacher worried about helping children to be comfortable writing and sharing their work, and as a researcher interested in the sense different children were making of the workshop. Was it important that Ken was a popular, middle class boy, and Karen a quiet, unpopular, working class girl? Was it important that Ken and Karen were two black children in a predominantly white classroom? My role as a teacher probably contributed to Karen's seeming interpretation of my words as scolding. Questions like, "Why did you do that?" asked out in the hall by an adult and teacher, may very well signify to a student that she is in trouble.

But more important than issues of access to information and its connection to the teacher role, is that children bring to the classroom playground and cafeteria experiences, individual and collective histories in and out of school, that contribute to their evaluations of each other as friends and audiences. As teachers of any particular group of children, we have limited control over important aspects of peer relations. I am certainly not saying that we can do nothing to influence or enhance these relationships. Only that, at any given moment, children are working out their relations with each other, and they are doing it from their pasts, behind our backs, and outside the room, as well as within situations we have greater access to and upon which we exert greater influence.

Consider Jil, who mentioned James, among others, as someone she did not want to work with ("ever") in the writing workshop. After also rejecting John as an audience in peer conferences ("He's biting me, he's scratching me, he's throwing his pencil"), she said:

JIL: Um, Robert, Suzanne, James, William, um, David, Ken, did I mention Suzanne?
INTR: Mm hm. Why do you not like to work with them?
JIL: They tease me all the time, they're my (inaudible). I will never, I haven't liked them since I met them and I will never like them. (Interview, 5-23-90)

A common, often accurate, prediction made by teachers at Clifford on pleasant, warm mornings was that the children would come into school worked up and difficult to handle. The reasoning was that children tended to come to school earlier on nice days and have more time outside with each other before class started. This often led to fights, which came into school with children as they began their school day.

A second theme of this chapter, then, is how the routine and norms of the writing workshop helped and hindered children in their efforts to work and share their texts with desirable audiences. The openness of writing time in the workshop routine (as well as Grace's presence) allowed me to arrange for a sharing session for Karen with a small group of children she appeared to have trusted. But Ken also took advantage of this openness, and chose to join us there. Ken's freedom of movement affected Karen's experience in the sharing session. The writing workshop gave children access to each other, and this appears to have been, for most children, a mixed blessing.

In my story of James and his friends, I told how important peers were to their experiences within the classroom. James collaborated with one or more of his friends throughout the year, and placed great value on his peers' comments in peer conferences (to the point that he seemed to worry more about pleasing them than me). Although he expressed some apprehension about reading his work in front of girls who he thought probably did not like him and his stories, he clearly relished the opportunity to perform for the class during sharing time.

But other children had greatly different experiences in the workshop, and defined themselves quite differently in relation to peer audiences in collaborative work, peer conferences, and sharing sessions. Perhaps the greatest contrast is provided by Jessie, who largely rejected peers as audiences for her work (with, from what I could tell, good reason).

Jessie was the classroom's "female pariah" (Thorne, 1986), ostracized by nearly everyone "by virtue of gender, but also through some added stigma such as being overweight or poor" (p. 175). Jessie was not small, and she came from the trailer park. Nearly everyone in the class, in their interviews, said that she was the least popular person in the class, and the least desirable with whom to work. Bruce, for example, called her "idiotic, dumb," John said that she stunk, and Mary that she never brushed her teeth. Only a few children—Janis, Karen, Jil—said that they had worked with her in the class. Grace and I often intervened in verbal fights between Jessie and other children (I discuss one such incident that occurred before school in the next chapter). Jessie was by no means a passive victim—she fought back (and started a few fights herself) with volume and sarcasm.

In her interview, Jessie said that she had only a few friends in the class—Janis and Karen—and a few others in the other third grade class. She said she sometimes conferenced with Janis and Karen and shared her finished pieces with them, but usually she kept her work to herself. When asked, "Who do you write for?" she said, "Um, myself. I just write for myself. Or sometimes I'd write a story to somebody, and let them read it" (Interview, 5-30-90). Although she published four books across the year, she did not share her books either during sharing time or in the writing workshop library. She did often conference with me, Grace, and the teacher aide. In contrast to James and his friends, she seemed to look much more to adults than peers as audiences. For example, when asked what she did not like about the workshop, she said, "Some times I didn't like it was when Mr. Lensmire couldn't get to me [for a writing conference]. I didn't like that." Another interesting bit of evidence for the importance of adult audiences for Jessie came during her interview: Of all the children interviewed, Jessie was the only one who insisted that the interviewer talk to her a second time so that she could read her stories to the interviewer. Other children occasionally read and discussed their work in interviews—Jessie ended up reading and commenting upon three of her four published stories in an extra half hour session with her interviewer.

Several other children seemed similarly oriented toward adults as audiences rather than peers. Karen, for example, gave a surprising answer (at least in relation to other children's answers) to the question used to gain information about what peers she liked to work with in the room:

INTR: Who are the people in your class that you like to be with and work with?
KAREN: Um, my teachers. (Interview, 5-21-90)

Later, Karen expanded her answer to "sometimes my friends." Karen also looked outside the classroom for an important audience. When describing what she did with one of her texts after it had been published, she said that she read it over first, went home, and "I give it to my mom and she reads it and then she'll probably say, 'that's good, very nice, very nice.'" Sharing her work with peers did not appear in her story of what she did with her published work. When asked who she wrote for, she replied, "Me, Mommy, and some people."

Janis, a friend of Karen and Jessie, talked about teacher and peer conferences in ways that were almost perfectly opposed to the ways James discussed them. James had said that he sometimes took my advice on his writing, depending on his own assessment of its worth. But, at least in his interview, he gave peers' advice much more weight, saying that he would change his text if two peers said they did not like something. Janis, on the same topics:

INTR: If he [Mr. Lensmire] gave you advice or a suggestion on how to make things better, did you always follow his advice?
JANIS: Yes I did.
INTR: How did you feel about the conferences with Mr. Lensmire, did they help you become a better writer?
JANIS: Yes, they did and I felt good about them.

(Later)

Intr: Did you always use the advice of other classmates?
JANIS: Sometimes I did and sometimes I didn't.
INTR: And what made you choose, how did you decide?
JANIS: Well when a person's like, why don't you add on to the story like make it, make it more adventurous and that made me go ahead and make it more adventurous, but when a person said why don't you

cut down the adventure and make it more dramatic, and I'd say no,
I don't want to do that. (Interview, 5-21-90)

And John, a student teased perhaps as much as or more than Jessie,
said that he liked talking to teachers better than students about his
papers. When asked why, he said:

JOHN: Well, I trust teachers.
INTR: Really? You can't trust students?
JOHN: No.
INTR: How come?
JOHN: Because they're younger. (Interview, 5-21-90)

John later linked his preference for teachers to what teachers knew,
saying, "Because the kids, I, the kids don't know as much." One interpretation of John's comments is that he preferred older, wiser teachers,
perhaps with a certain disrespect for what other children know and their
value as an audience. His comments, then, might be interpreted as
expressing something which traditional, teacher-centered pedagogy
often ends up doing—encouraging children to not trust themselves or
other children as sources of knowledge and insight.

But we need to take John's first comment—"I trust teachers"—more
seriously. A common response by children to John's work in sharing sessions was that they could not understand his stories. They would voice
these complaints in ways that made it difficult for me to decide if com-
prehension of John's often difficult, adventuresome texts was the problem, or if it was just an excuse for giving him a hard time. Suzanne, who
John claimed often "tormented" him, hinted at both of these possibilities
in her interview. First she said that John was "smarter than the rest of us
and doesn't really make sense to the rest of us." Then, "he doesn't know
how to write right, I don't think . . . he just doesn't explain his words,
his sentences too good." Later, she linked children teasing John to not
understanding his work: "a lot of people tease him and say I don't understand the writing, I don't like the writing." Finally, when asked why children teased John and said that they did not understand or like his writing, she replied, "He is really obnoxious" (Interview, 5-18-90). Her
responses suggest that criticism of John's work might have had as much
to do with children's perceptions of John as it did with their perceptions
of his texts.

My own interpretation of John's comments, above, is that he could
trust teachers as audiences for his texts because they brought more

knowledge and patience than peers to his texts *and to him*. He was more confident, with teachers, that he would be understood—his texts comprehended and appreciated, but also understood in terms of an acceptance of him as a writer and a child.

Despite their relative preference for teachers as audiences, both Janis and John reported conferencing and collaborating (occasionally) with other children. They also were frequent readers during sharing sessions. Jessie was not. She had decided that it was too risky to share her stories with most of her peers in conferences, sharing time, and the workshop library. After identifying children with whom she did not want to conference, Jessie described how she would feel if she were forced to conference with them:

INTR: What would they do with your writing? How would you feel if you
    had to conference with them?
JESSIE: I would feel like a jar of slime. Being sat on.
INTR: So maybe they don't treat you very well?
JESSIE: Yes. No, like getting cut in half. (Interview, 5-30-90)

Later, she said that she never shared in front of the whole class because they would make her feel the same way in that situation (she resisted several attempts by me to have her share, as Karen did, with small groups of friends). Her description of how her peers would accomplish making her feel "cut in half" during a sharing session surprised me. I had expected her to predict verbal attacks on her work when she finished sharing a story. Instead:

Because, cause, for some people, it, nobody would, would um, *answer*, or *ask them questions*. I know that. (Interview, 5-30-90; my emphasis)

Jessie feared silence, a rejection expressed not with words but with no words, when there were supposed to be words; an active silence. Jessie's comments assumed aspects of the sharing session that Grace and I had worked hard to put in place. If an author asked her classmates for specific help in relation to the piece she was reading, then we expected children to respond to the author's request in their response before going on to other topics—"nobody would answer." If the author did not set up the sharing session this way, we expected children to first talk with the author about what they liked, and then move to questions that they had about the work—"or ask them questions."

From the beginning, I worked to make the writing workshop, and its conferences and sharing times, a safe place for children to write and share their work. In the opening meeting of the 2nd day of the workshop, I talked about risk and the need for a supportive audience:

> I talked about how confusing things might be for a while, that the writing workshop was going to be different because writing demanded invention, rather than learning what somebody else was saying (I rushed this). I said that two important things authors do is write about things that they care about and that they take risks.
>
> I then gave some examples of students who had already taken risks. I started with William, who I had talked to the day before when he said he had nothing to write about. I said that he had taken a risk and wrote a rough draft even though he didn't know how to spell every single word. I told them that that was fine in a rough draft, that they could worry about spelling later if they wanted to publish the piece. I watched William as I said this—I wondered if I embarrassed him when I wanted to compliment him. Later, he came up to me and said that he had spelled all the words wrong. But it seemed like he was trying to strike up a conversation, rather than beating himself up after my comment. He said that tomorrow he was going to write about baseball, so I don't think he is too damaged. I said that John, in his piece, "Me," had taken risks, since he was writing a sort of autobiography. I said that maybe he should read it to the class—he said he would when he was finished. Finally, I said that Robert (is that his name?—black hair, crew cut, round face) had taken a risk when he wrote about something sad. I said that we would have to respect him and not make him feel embarrassed if he wanted to read his story to us. He seemed pleased, and told me later that he was drawing a picture to go along with his story.
>
> At the end of my little lecture, I said that if we were going to be authors, we needed a safe place to write. To have a safe place, we needed to respect one another and be patient with one another. I told them that we would work on ways to help and support each other as writers. (Fieldnotes, 8-31-89)

As the year progressed, we did many activities to help children respond to each other's writing in helpful ways. Grace and I held "peer" conferences in front of the class in which we talked with each other about our own writing; I led discussions of student texts I had placed on the overhead; children role-played peer conferences in front of the class, which we then discussed and assessed; we developed guidelines for response that children kept in their writing folders:

1. Find a spot away from the quiet zone.
2. The author reads out loud.

3. The listener responds: tell the author what you liked. Tell the author what you remember about her writing. Tell the author what you thought was interesting.
4. The listener asks some questions about the author's writing: let the author teach you about his topic.
5. The author and listener talk about what to do next. Will the author make changes? How will she do it?

Grace and I were quite active, at times, in sharing sessions, both reminding children before we started that we needed to respect and support our fellow writers, and intervening during sharing sessions when children seemed unsupportive. Perhaps Jessie's fear of silence reflected her knowledge of the active role we took during sharing—she may have known we would address hurtful student comments, but she was less sure (as I am) that we could address *no* comments, no answers or questions.

Obviously, these teacher efforts were not enough to make the classroom a safe place for Jessie to share her texts with peers. Jessie's peers were a significant part of her not feeling safe. When asked why other people felt comfortable sharing their stories in front of class, Jessie said, "Because they have lots of friends."

———

Jessie systematically avoided peer audiences in peer conferences, sharing sessions, and the workshop library. Most children in the room, however, reported that they *sought and avoided* specific peer audiences in their daily interactions in the classroom. A primary way children accomplished this was in their selection of who they peer conferenced with on their texts. Some of the patterns documented in the chapter on James and his friends characterized the workshop as a whole. *Children conferenced with friends within gender boundaries.* All children identified other children they did and did not want to conference with—in other words, they made inclusions and exclusions, and these differentiations were, as with James and friends, at times associated with social class and gender differences. Karen, for example, spoke for boys and girls when she stated that "the boys like the boys, but the girls like the girls" for peer conferences (Interview, 5-21-90). In Mary and Lori's interview, Mary was quite explicit about who she did and did not want to work with: "I like working with Carol, Lisa, Marie, Sharon, Emily, Julie, and Suzanne. And I don't like working with the boys." Mary's list of girls, except possibly for Emily and Julie, is a fairly complete naming of the most popular girls in the class. She also was forthcoming about girls she did not want to work with, and why. Mary said that "some of them had lice, they stunk," she did not like their "styles" or their personalities.

MARY: Most of them, and some of them are from the trailer park and I don't like working with people who are from the trailer park. . . . Like at first I thought that Lori was from the trailer park before I went over to her house the first time.
LORI: Thanks a lot.
MARY: Well I did. (Interview, 5-31-90)

But friendship and trust (or lack of it) were the most common reasons given for their decisions, especially when children were asked why they did not want to work with certain children. I reported in the last chapter that Bruce did not want to work with James because he could not trust him to keep secrets about his stories. James had expressed apprehension about conferencing and sharing his texts with girls in the class because he believed they would not like his work, and assumed that they did not like him. Robert, one of the boys from the trailer park of whom James was critical, said in his interview that he had conferenced with Leon, his "friend William," and Rajesh. When asked why he conferenced with them, he responded:

ROBERT: Well, I know they wouldn't like tell everybody, you know?
INTR: No, tell me. Tell everybody what?
ROBERT: Well, they wouldn't tell, they wouldn't go off telling everybody what you wrote.
INTR: Yeah. Is that important to you?
ROBERT: Yes it is.
INTR: Why is that?
ROBERT: Well, because, sometimes they laugh at you, they tease you.
INTR: What do they laugh or tease you about?
ROBERT: Well, what you didn't write and what they didn't write, like the same, like, they would think that theirs, theirs was better than the others. (Interview, 5-24-90)

Marie, one of the more popular girls in class, said that she did not want to read her pieces to "people who pick on me, make fun of me," because they "probably would say, that story is bad, and stuff, they'd try to make fun of stuff" (Interview, 5-16-90).

Marie's use of "probably would say," instead of something like, "they said that," is indicative of children's reports of their experiences in

peer conferences. Although *almost no children* reported bad experiences in peer conferences, most *anticipated* bad experiences if they
conferenced with certain children. The few exceptions focused on difficulties children had working with another person on writing, not with
instances of children teasing or hurting each other in conferences.
Rajesh, for example, reported getting into arguments with other children
as he tried to revise texts with them. Rajesh refers below, I think, to
moving a bit of text around to see where it should go (I had showed
children how to cut up and physically manipulate their rough drafts during revision):

> Why would I get into arguments? Because, I was like just really mad,
> I was like, why don't we put it here, and he was like, no, no, no, no,
> it was right here, here, here. (Interview, 5-18-90)

I partly attribute the success of peer conferences—success in terms
of their being safe interactions—to the work Grace and I did to help children interact in positive, supportive ways. But I attribute much of their
success to children's opportunities to select their first audiences in peer
conferences and collaborations during writing time. The norms of this
part of the workshop routine, especially the relative freedom of movement and association, granted children an opportunity that we adult writers often take for ourselves: It gave them the chance to share texts with
friendly, trusted audiences before sending them on to, perhaps, less
friendly ones.

But as I noted in relation to Karen's sharing session at the beginning of this chapter, and as should be apparent from the previous
chapter and some of Jessie and Robert's comments above, the openness of writing time made it difficult for children to avoid sometimes
hostile texts, talk, and audiences. Outside the purview of the teachers'
influence, there was writing used to tease classmates: When asked if
children ever used writing to tease one another, Bruce replied, "Yeah,
but they, but then they crumpled it up and threw it away" (Interview,
5-21-90). There was underground talk: In the last chapter, remember,
Sharon and Carol told about trying to get their names out of boys' stories, and then suggested that even if they succeeded (often with the
help of the teacher), the boys could keep them "in" the story orally, by
telling their friends who the characters really were. And children could
read a child's story over his back when he did not want them to, did
not ask for their comments: "You were writing, they'd come over to
your desk and they, they say like their story's so big and neat" (Robert,
Interview, 5-24-90).

Writing time gave children the chance to connect with people with whom they needed or wanted to connect. It also provided opportunities for confrontation, fighting, and teasing. Furthermore, except when such problems made themselves known—by being loud, named by a child, accidently or purposefully observed by teachers—I had limited access to and influence over these interactions. This was a risk I was taking as a teacher in order for children to have access to each other when they needed it and wanted it.

Sharing time also made it difficult for children to avoid undesirable peer audiences. The most common form sharing time took was an individual author reading her text to the entire class. After some of the children's comments above, perhaps it seems unlikely that anyone would want to share under such circumstances. But actually, many children did share pieces with the class, and reported it being, overall, a positive experience (if a little scary) in their interviews. Of course, as I have already noted, some children did not want to share, and sometimes children would ask friends to read their texts to the class—they would stand next to or behind the author's chair as their friends read their texts. Karen, Emily, and others did this.

I tried, with Grace, to make these sharing sessions safe places for children to read and receive response from their classmates. I drew heavily on Graves (1983) and Calkins (1986), and other workshop advocates, for guidance in how to go about this in the classroom. But workshop advocates overestimate, as I did, the extent to which teachers can smooth over peer conflict with interventions such as teacher modeling of response and rules for behavior. Imagine Rajesh coming to the writing workshop after being pushed around by James and Bruce on the playground. What sort of audience for his texts are James and Bruce, *whatever their in-class behavior?*

If they tell Rajesh, very politely, during sharing time, that they did not understand the meaning of parts of his story, what does that mean? What does it mean for Rajesh? What does it mean to me, as the teacher, especially if I do not know that Rajesh got pushed around at recess? Does it mean that they were genuinely puzzled by Rajesh's story and offered their observations in hopes that it would help him improve his text? Or were their questions a subtle put down, voiced, of course, in appropriate language and tone, that made fun of Rajesh and his story? How do I know? Carol and Sharon said in their interview that James would not ask questions about boys' stories, but did ask them about girls' stories. They believed he did this to tease girls. In other words, even the mere presence and absence of seemingly appropriate responses might be meaningful (and hurtful).

These children had histories, individual and collective. They were working out relations continuously, in and out of the workshop, in and out of school. As a teacher, it was difficult to learn about these relations, to follow them, understand their significance for what was (and was not) said and written in the classroom. I had invited these relations in, had wanted to give them bigger play. I had hoped to capitalize on the interest and value children placed in each other as friends, as authors, and as audiences.

Because of my efforts—and despite them—peers were at once trusted and risky audiences for each other. In the next chapter, I discuss the writing of fiction as a response, in part, to risky peer audiences. Before I do, however, I want to tell one more story of a child sharing texts with peers, and then briefly examine the writing situation children faced in the writing workshop. The story is about John and his interactions with multiple audiences—in this case, peers, teachers, and even the principal. It demonstrates some of the difficulties I encountered and the errors I made in my attempts to understand and influence peer relations. The story reminds us that writing is risky, involves an exposure of self that can leave us vulnerable.

Robert provides an appropriate introduction to John's story. Robert said that he was "very nervous" about sharing his first published book in front of the class (he was one of the first children to do so):

ROBERT: And I, I didn't know what they were going to do.
INTR: Who?
ROBERT: The people, I thought that they were going to boo it and all that stuff.
INTR: Did they?
ROBERT: No, no. You never know what's going to happen. (Interview, 2-24-90)

Indeed.

> John shared a story today. As Grace said later, the workshop had been going fairly smoothly up to that point. Most kids were calm and writing (or at least looking like they were writing).
>
> John shared his piece. He has a certain presence when he shares. He seems very self-assured, not very nervous. He takes his time reading, shows his pictures slowly to the class, first to the right side, then middle and left, slowly rotating his body. He seemed so comfortable today that his pacing seemed a little slow—especially since the illustrations were too small for the kids in the back of the room to see anyway. I saw Carol turn to Marie several times and raise her eyebrows in what I interpreted as a sort of do-you-believe-this-guy look. Maya also made eye-contact with Carol while John was reading with a similar facial expression.

I had conferenced with John about the piece—it had been confusing, but I thought the part he added helped explain things. I really wasn't thinking any of this would create a problem.

After John finished sharing, I started clapping (as has become the custom), and several children joined me. John stopped us, saying he hadn't shown the final illustration yet. I don't know who started the questioning, but soon Suzanne, seated just to John's left in the first seat of the middle row, became the point person for a group of at least three—Carol, Maya, and Suzanne—telling John that they didn't understand his story. I quickly moved up to the front of the room, near John. I squatted down next to him as he sat in the author's chair. I put my right arm around him. I guess, more or less instinctively, I wanted to be by John and support him as he got some hard questions, possibly tinged with a little malice. I considered stopping sharing, but I wanted to continue. On the one hand, this might have been a sort of attack on John, coming from people who he often fought with (especially Suzanne). On the other hand, what they were saying was true in some sense, and I thought that it might be helpful to John to hear what they couldn't understand.

So, I went up by John. With my arm around him, I asked his respondents to respect him and be nice in their responses. Suzanne started again—she even said something like "no offense" and "I'm sorry if I offended you," which struck me as a little funny—and proceeded to say she didn't understand the story and that it had a "nothing" ending. A nothing ending—I can't remember how she explained it. Carol and Maya offered responses around Suzanne's, and added that his previous work suffered from similar problems. John tried to respond, more or less defending his piece, and I did the same, trying to keep them specific and stop them from exaggerating.

We were quite engaged. Then, at one point, I had to hold John in his seat—my supportive arm became a restraining one—I thought he was going to jump up and hit Suzanne or Maya. I quickly stopped sharing time, saying that perhaps John, Suzanne, Maya, and Carol could have a small group discussion some time if they wanted. I was thinking that this might be less threatening to John, and the girls would have less of an audience to nail John in front of (if that is what they were trying to do). John went to his seat, and I started telling the class to get ready for their next class with Grace as I walked down the middle aisle to the back of the room.

I turned around in time to see John jump out of his desk, rush Maya and then Suzanne, and pound each one of them on the hand with his fist. I trotted up to hold John. This was when the fireworks began (or the first explosion anyway). John and Suzanne were struggling with each other—a constant verbal struggle as well as grabbing each other and trying to scratch each other. Soon Grace and I were both in on the dance. At one point John and Suzanne were locked to one another, each not letting go of the other, and Grace and I were each holding a kid (Grace-Suzanne, me-John) trying to pry them apart. It was a circus—almost funny, since here were two adults, I think both not trying to yell too loud and not trying to handle the struggling kids too roughly. But the children were thoroughly engaged with each other. That's probably not very accurate. John was immersed (over his head). Suzanne was in control—she knew how to score off John. John was basically out of control. What I like about Suzanne—her sharp wit, her perception, her courage—were put to use against John, and he was no match.

Eventually, John and I went out into the hall. I just wanted to let John cool down. Carol told me later that Grace talked with the class about how scary it could be to share, and how the class would have to do a better job at making the author feel comfortable and supported. Meanwhile, I was out in the hall with John. The principal, Bill, just happened to be nearby. John was a little hot yet—I wanted to calm him down, tell him it wasn't just his fault, and apologize for not stopping things sooner.

Bill came over. I didn't feel it was necessary, but he must have. I quickly tried to explain what had happened. John interrupted with yells and bursts. Bill put his hands on John's shoulders, trying to get John to settle down. This was when the next round of trouble started. Bill told John to quiet down, that he was disturbing other classes (I doubt it). John responded with "I'm just telling you how I'm feeling," again quite loud. This escalated—Bill citing rules of politeness, John expressing his feelings—until John said, "Sometimes I think that you are a bad principal."

Bill had been standing in front of John, bent over at the waist. Now he put each of his hands on each side of John's face to talk to him. He was calm. He told John, with his face about three inches from John's, that he had the choice of settling down and being quiet or going to the office with him where Bill would call his parents to have him taken home. John is not very good at being silent, especially when he is agitated. He again said—not quite a shout, but loud enough—that he was just saying how he was feeling. Bill, who was very serious, but not enraged or anything like that, simply said, "That's it," and started walking to the office with John, holding his hand.

What has happened? A small child—a third grader—shared his book in front of the class. A small group of children who probably don't like John (Suzanne told me later that day that John really bugs her) criticized his work as not being understandable. They not only criticized this text, but also named two or three others, saying that all of his work is like this. As a teacher, I made an error in thinking that something constructive could come of this—I intervened, tried to support John, get his critics to be more specific and help John (Ha!) understand specifically what they don't understand. Out of this—an engaging, vital discussion, I suppose—John got in trouble with the principal (when things matter in schools, bad things can happen; honesty—John was being very honest throughout—doesn't necessarily do well in school).

I followed John to the principal's office. I didn't want John to get in all sorts of trouble. I went into the office with them, and quickly explained that John had been sharing a story, and that Suzanne and some others had criticized his piece, and that he and Suzanne had gotten into an "argument." Bill's line with John was that he had to control himself. John's consistent line was that he was just saying how he felt. I really admired John. Here was this little third grader, sitting in the principal's office with two adults, and he wasn't backing down or cowering—he was much calmer by now, which made things easier for Bill, I think.

Then, just when I thought this all was about over, John pursued the "bad principal" thing again. He made both a more general and specific critique, saying that kids, not just him, thought that Bill was a bad principal because all he did was say hi to them sometimes. Now I felt a little bad for Bill—my presence might make this harder for him to take than if it was just John and him. But Bill handled it well. He told John that he thought John had said what he did because John was angry. John eventually apologized on his own, sort of—he said that he was frustrated and said what he said when he was angry. But he never said that what he said wasn't true. It didn't seem to matter to Bill. I took John back to the classroom.

Before we left, I told Bill, in front of John, that he might want to talk to Suzanne, since she had been part of this as well. I didn't really want Bill to talk to her, but I wanted John to know that we weren't coming down only on him. Bill has had many dealings with Suzanne—she seems to get in a lot of fights before school. He said that he would talk to her sometime at lunch.

Before I took John into class, I apologized to him. I told him that it was partly my fault for letting things get as far as they did, and that I shouldn't have let Suzanne and the others criticize his work that way. I told him that I thought his revision had made his story much better, and that his other work was really very good work (the truth). At issue here for me—I want John to keep exploring, to keep taking risks, and not write boring, more understandable stuff because of what some children who don't like him anyway say about his work. John said that it wasn't my fault at all, and walked into the classroom. (Fieldnotes, 3-25-90)

Elbow (1987) relates how, when struggling for words in speaking situations, he often involuntarily closes his eyes. He interprets this behavior as an "instinctive attempt to blot out awareness of audience when I need all my concentration for just trying to figure out or express what I want to say" (p. 50). From this personal start, he goes on to examine different rhetorics and psychologies, and their implications for the manipulation of audience, by teachers of writing, for the benefit of student writers. Elbow is concerned that current theories and practices put too much emphasis and faith in audience awareness, and ignore how audiences can push back on writing and make it defensive, tangled, absent.

Elbow argues that two "pieties of composition theory" are often in conflict. One, from the classical rhetorical tradition, would have writers think about audience as they write. The other, which Elbow associates with a "newer epistemic tradition" grounded in the work of Berthoff, encourages writers to use writing to make new meaning—and, as Elbow notes, "it's often difficult to work out new meaning while thinking about readers" (p. 53).

This conflict is visible in my fieldnotes of John's sharing session, especially toward the end of the notes. I am worried that John will lose his creativity and uniqueness if he bends his work too much to peer audiences. But my words and actions, that day at least, functioned to force John to face his audience—keep his eyes open, even as I tried to support him and shape audience response. (At various times earlier in the year, I had John read to older children in Clifford school—according to John, these sessions were quite successful.) I wrote that "it might be helpful to John" if he understood what his peers did not understand about his piece. In other words, I wanted to socialize John, and use his peers to do it.

My stance has support from current psychological models:

> From one side, the Piagetians say, in effect, "The egocentric little critters, we've got to socialize 'em. Ergo, make them think about audience when they write!" From the other side, the Vygotskians say, in effect, "No wonder they're having trouble writing. They've been bamboozled by Piagetian heresy. They think they're solitary individuals with private selves when really they're just congeries of voices that derive from their discourse community. Ergo, let's intensify the social context—use peer groups and publication: make them think about audience when they write. (Elbow, 1987, p. 57)

The image of me crouching with my arm around John as he sat in the author's chair is a powerful representation of the writing situation children faced in the writing workshop. My arm around John was both supportive and coercive. I used it to express solidarity with John, so that he knew he was not alone in a difficult writing/speaking situation. I also used my arm to keep him in the situation, a situation constructed of talk, rather than let him transform the situation by possibly expressing his frustration or disappointment physically (or was he just trying to run away?). As far as I can tell, I was a safe audience for John and most children in the room, even preferred by some over peers. I worked to help them find topics and purposes for their writing; I supported their efforts. At the same time, I made them write, and in a social situation in which peers were purposefully prominent audiences.

One of the responses children made to the presence of multiple peer audiences in the writing workshop was similar to Elbow "closing his eyes." They avoided certain peer audiences and turned to other ones for support. These alternative audiences were other peers, teachers, sometimes parents.

Writing is risky, and children in the workshop experienced this to a greater or lesser degree. An important part of what made writing risky to them was sharing their work with peers. In this, these third graders joined other writers in their ambivalent relations with audiences. On the one hand, we risk exposing ourselves and our work to criticism when we share it with others. On the other hand, audiences are sources of support, and we often write exactly because we want others to read our texts—sharing our work is part of a communicative transaction in written language. Richards (1986), a professional sociologist and writer, discusses risk in these terms:

> For me, sitting down to write is risky because it means that I have to open myself up to scrutiny. . . . Every piece of work can be used as evidence about what kind of a sociologist (and person) you are. . . . I cannot face the possibility of people thinking I'm stupid. (pp. 113, 114)

Audiences are sources of risk in the chance that they will reject the work and the author. But audiences are also sources of affirmation, of encouragement, that cannot be tapped until something is written and shared.

> So there I am, faced with the blank page, confronting the risk of discovering that I cannot do what I want to do, and therefore am not the person I pretend to be. I haven't yet written anything, so no one can help me affirm my commitment and underscore my sense of who I am. (p. 117)

Richards "solves" this problem much like my students did in the workshop—by sharing her work, especially her working drafts, with people she trusts, people she has a common history with, who have seen "early attempts to write and think . . . and believed there was something lurking there beneath all the confusion" (p. 116). This does not remove risk—other audiences may be on the horizon, we may still worry about sharing texts even with trusted friends, may still fail to do what we had hoped in our writing—but it often helps us to write, to risk.

But we should not forget John in the author's chair. Children in the workshop were often confronted by audiences with whom they were less than comfortable. Furthermore, they *had* to write. If they wanted to do as their teacher asked, the blank page could not remain blank for long, whatever the risk of exposure they felt. So they wrote, and worked to collaborate and share their texts with friends. And for most, the situation seemed to be quite satisfactory, assuming (as Jessie did not) that you had "lots of friends."

Chapter 5

Fiction, Distance, and Control

LENSMIRE: Emily, why do you think that everybody in the class writes fiction, instead of writing like, you wrote a couple stories that were really about yourself, you know, like you and your dog and stuff like that. But most people write fiction.

EMILY: Well, it's probably because they really make up things to make it more interesting, that's, it's mostly why they, it's mostly why they write about different people, like James, the story he wrote about Lisa.

LENSMIRE: Uh huh.

EMILY: Well he, like, I think he just wanted to have the story more interesting.

LENSMIRE: More interesting than what? So, are you saying that stuff that happens to people isn't interesting?

EMILY: Well, not really, but if you make it more exciting like sort of add more things to it, it can be kind of interesting, it's not—

LENSMIRE: Do you, I've been wondering if you think sometimes people are a little bit afraid of, of talking about themselves in front of classmates, and so they—

EMILY: Yeah, that's, that's mostly it. They're probably afraid of talking about themselves.

LENSMIRE: You think so? I mean, you don't have to believe what I say.

EMILY: Yeah, that's, that's what I thought at the beginning because no, mostly nobody was writing about themselves, they were writing about, stories about like, James, he wrote about Lisa and Kurt.

LENSMIRE: Did, so you think that they're, you think they're, some kids just don't want to write about—

EMILY: They're just scared that people will laugh at them because they're writing about themselves.

LENSMIRE: So, how, why did you have the guts to write about something that really happened to you?

EMILY: It, it was so much, so interesting that I didn't want to just keep it in all my life and not talk about it. (Audiotape, 3-29-90)

Near the end of my teaching in the writing workshop, I became especially interested in how risks associated with writing were related to the writing children did in the classroom. A week and a half before the above conversation with Emily, I had asked, in my fieldnotes, "who writes personal narratives?" as I puzzled through the incongruence between the topics and stories I discussed with James, Ken, and Bruce in writing conferences, and what they actually wrote about in the workshop (Fieldnotes, 3-19-90). In these notes and others like them, I named and brought to my own attention an aspect of the writing children did in the room that I had noticed before, but had not seriously considered: Almost all the texts children wrote, and especially those they published, were fictional narratives. And this was despite the fact that, in whole group activities and writing conferences across the year, I had consistently attempted to help them identify and write about topics and stories that rather directly expressed their own experiences.

In what follows, I argue that fictional narratives offered children several advantages over personal narratives and other topics and genres. One advantage fiction offered was distance. By writing fiction, children could avoid directly exposing themselves and their experiences and values to the scrutiny of peers and teachers. Above, Emily said that children were "just scared that people will laugh at them because they're about themselves." A second advantage was control. Children seemed to value fiction for the control it gave them over their material. Emily noted that writers of fiction could "make it more interesting." Children felt less restricted by their material, felt they could shape their texts in ways that would please their audiences, and felt that fiction was more enjoyable to write than nonfiction. Fiction helped children avoid risks associated with the presence of more and less trusted audiences in the classroom, and allowed them to manipulate their material in ways that satisfied their audiences and themselves as writers.

———

I used the handout reproduced in Figure 5.1 with children early in the year to help them find things to write about. I did not expect that they

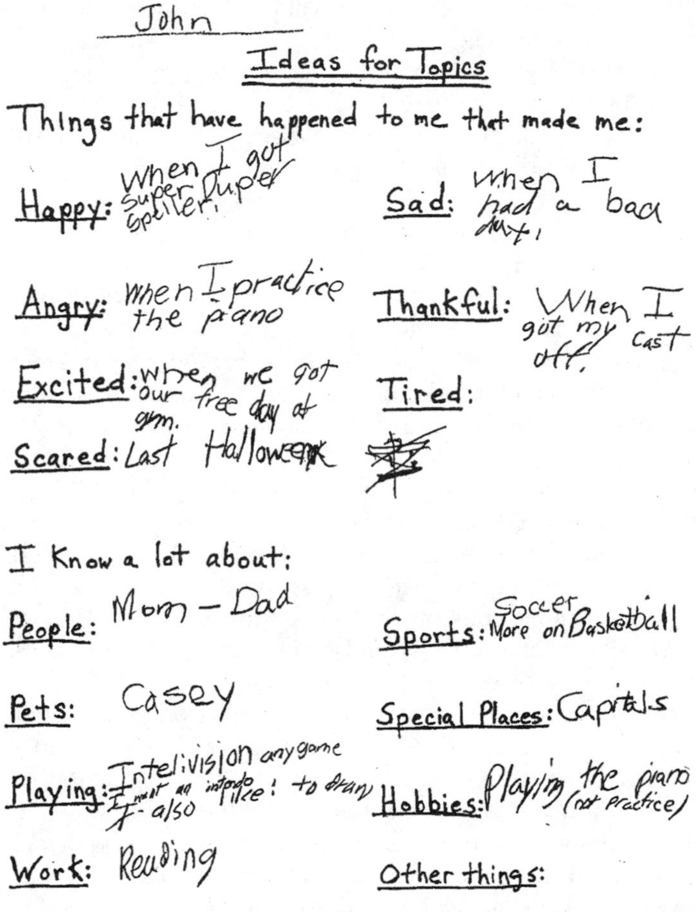

John

Ideas for Topics

Things that have happened to me that made me:

Happy: When I got super duper speller!

Sad: When I had a bad day.

Angry: When I practice the piano

Thankful: When I got my cast off.

Excited: When we got our free day at gym.

Tired:

Scared: Last Halloween

I know a lot about:

People: Mom – Dad

Sports: Soccer More on Basketball

Pets: Casey

Special Places: Capitals

Playing: Intelivision any game I'm not an impedo! to draw I also like

Hobbies: Playing the piano (not practice)

Work: Reading

Other things:

Figure 5.1. Ideas for Topics handout.

would fill in all the spaces, only that they would use the sheet as a tool for identifying stories to tell and meaningful topics about which to write. The handout captures, in fairly stark fashion, the type of writing I was encouraging children to do—writing that Britton (1978, 1982) would label "expressive." Temple et al. (1988), with reference to Britton, characterize expressive language as

> Language that is close to the self, used to reveal the nature of the person, to verbalize his consciousness, and to exhibit his close relation to the reader. Expressive language is a free flow of ideas and feelings. (p. 131)

In addition to the expressive function, Britton (1978) identifies two other functions that language can serve: transactional and poetic. Language serving a transactional function is used to do something: inform, persuade, solve problems, or theorize. Within the transactional function "an utterance . . . is a means to some end outside itself, and its organization will be the principle of efficiency in carrying out that end" (p. 18). In contrast, language serving the poetic function is used to create something with words. In this function, language itself becomes the focus of attention, as when we gossip, tell stories, or write novels for the enjoyment and satisfaction they give us as verbal objects.

Expressive writing often precedes, in a child's developmental history, writing in transactional and poetic modes (Temple et al., 1988). Within such a conception of writing development, children gradually gain control over their expressive writing and shape it toward the demands of transactional and poetic functions, as well as continue writing for expressive purposes. This progression can be used to characterize a child's overall writing development, but can also be used to characterize the history of individual texts. As writers, we may identify important themes and stories for future development through expressive writing, with writing that is "informal or casual, loosely structured" (Britton, 1978, p. 18)—perhaps by brainstorming, writing letters to friends, by doing some "free writing" (Elbow, 1973). And then, we may gradually build on and manipulate these earlier texts, and shape them toward more public and formal ends in transactional and poetic discourses.

My teaching assumed similar progressions. The handout in Figure 5.1 anticipates poetic and transactional functions fairly directly, asking for stories (things that have happened) and topics that could be identified and gradually shaped toward poetic and transactional ends. But the handout begins with and emphasizes the expressive function. These stories will be things that happened to "me," topics that "I" know a lot about.

Many children noted problems with exactly this sort of expressive writing, exactly because it was "close to the self" and revealed the "nature of the person." Some commented, as Emily did above, on the risks of talking about yourself in front of classmates. Marie, for example, said that "maybe people would come up to me and start laughing at that," if she wrote about herself (Interview, 5-16-90). William wrote several stories about himself playing sports at the beginning of the year, but went on to publish only fiction. When I asked him about this, he responded:

WILLIAM: I don't know, people would probably laugh at me.
LENSMIRE: You think so?
WILLIAM: Yeah.

LENSMIRE: That's, I was always worried about that. So you, do you think other people felt that way in class?
WILLIAM: Maybe, maybe not. I don't really know.
LENSMIRE: Yeah, because some other people told me that they were scared to write about themselves because they were worried that other people would laugh at them or not like it.
WILLIAM: Me too. (Audiotape, 5-18-90)

Other children seemed less afraid of peer response, and more concerned with keeping private things private. In other words, fear seemed less a motivation than a wish to protect their privacy. Suzanne, a child who moved with power and confidence among children and her teachers, and who did occasionally write personal narratives, said that she did not like to write about herself because it was "too personal":

> Like if I were supposed to write about when I grew up, when I was born and things like that, sometimes I think that's personal. (Interview, 5-18-90)

But often, the wish to keep private things private was linked to a fear of exposure. Rajesh attributed such a fear to Jessie and her "bad past":

RAJESH: Because somebody might have had a real, a bad past, and so they didn't want to tell about that past and so they just want to write about fiction.
INTR: Don't you share things like that with—
RAJESH: Everybody, almost everybody in that class, including me, knew it.
INTR: So you don't think she [Jessie] would like to write about herself then?
RAJESH: Yeah, she just writes sequels of Sleeping Beauty. I mean, she is more in her own group. (Interview, 5-18-90)

In his last comment, Rajesh suggests the isolation Jessie experienced in this class: "she is more in her own group." He attributes to Jessie a "bad past," and gives this as a reason for her to write fiction instead of personal narratives. Rajesh was correct that Jessie wrote her own version of "Sleeping Beauty"—I discuss it at the end of this chapter—but he was incorrect in his suggestion that Jessie typically wrote fiction. Jessie published four books across the year. One of them was her retelling of "Sleeping Beauty," and another was a retelling of a scary story called "The Big Toe," that she found in a book from the school library. But two of her books were personal narratives: *Misty* told about adventures with her dog, and *My Friends* told the story of her rather rocky friendships in kindergarten and later grades with Jil, from this class, and Barbara, from the other third grade. One of the ironic "benefits" of Jessie's alienation from and rejection of her peers seems to have been the opportunity to write some important stories from her own past. In other words, one way to solve the problem of exposing yourself to peers was to not let them see your stories. In this, Jessie seemed to be following the advice Jil offered to children who were afraid to write about themselves. Jil believed "it was good to write about yourself. It's fine." If you were afraid of people making fun, "Keep it in a safe place, take it home, put it in a combination steel safe" (Interview, 5-23-90).

Most children, however, did not lock personal narratives away in a safe. Most children wrote and published fiction. Perhaps the easiest way to suggest the prevalence of fiction in the room is by categorizing and counting the books that children made available to each other by placing them in the writing workshop library. I have records of what books were checked out of the library from the sign-out book. Although there were probably a number of books that were never signed out officially— this all was rather informal and fluid—the list of books I compiled from the sign-out book should be fairly representative of the books in the library across the year. Of 21 books checked out of the library, representing 20 different student authors—some, such as *The Fake Line Leader* trilogy, were collaborations and some authors were represented by more than one book—17 were fictional narratives, 2 were personal narratives, 1 was an ABC book, and another a book of jokes.

In the workshop library, fictional narratives clearly outnumbered other genres. I have not tried to categorize and count all the rough drafts and texts children wrote during the year (I do not have all the drafts, and the effort is unnecessary for my purposes here), but my impression from watching the children write across the year and casually perusing their writing folders in preparation for this writing, is that there were more personal narratives, proportionately, written than would be suggested by the workshop library. Some children, such as William and Robert, wrote rough drafts of personal narratives they never published or shared; others, such as Suzanne, wrote and shared personal narratives in sharing time, but did not publish them; and still other children, such as Jessie, published personal narratives that they did not share with peers in the library or in sharing sessions. Of course, there were other genres written that were not represented in the library—poetry we often published by giving the poets ten photocopies of final versions for them to distribute to whom they wished; and Sharon, one of the authors not represented in the library, wrote a series of biographies of children and teachers in the room. Sharon read her work to classmates, and shared published work outside of the library.

The workshop library, however, is a good place to look for a sense of what sort of texts the children in this room valued. Children with books in the library made at least two major decisions that suggest the desirability of fictional narratives to them. One decision was to publish a specific rough draft, often from a number of other drafts. A second decision was to put the published piece in the library. In making these decisions (as well as in their decisions of what to write in the first place) most children chose fictional narratives.

One reason children chose and valued fictional narratives was the distance it afforded them. By writing fiction, they could avoid the close identification between author and story that personal narratives involved. Fictional narratives offered them a way to distance themselves from the experiences and values expressed in their stories. Britton (1982) discusses a key way this distance is accomplished:

> Literary discourse . . . IS concerned with the private thoughts and feelings of the writer, but in "bringing them out of hiding" he objectifies them and may explore them through the creation of a personae, so that "we cannot assume that when a literary writer uses the first person he is describing his own experiences or making a confession." (p. 158; quotations are from Widdowson, 1975)

Fiction lessened, for children, risks associated with self-exposure. As Britton notes above, we do not necessarily assume, when reading fiction, that an author's own experiences are being related in a direct way, or that the author is making a confession when telling a story. We assume that the writer is *creating*, making up characters (their experiences and values), events, and things, engaged in crafting an acceptable sort of lie. Authors of fiction tell, as David said in his interview, "fake stories" (5-25-90).

The distance that writing fiction accomplishes is similar to Elbow "closing his eyes" and Karen asking someone else to read her text to classmates—it involves placing something between author and audience so that the author does not have to confront them directly. In expressive writing, authors face their audiences in the fairly direct expression of their experiences and values in texts. One of James' comments about a problem he had while writing *The Fake Line Leader* seems particularly interesting in relation to this discussion:

> Yeah, in my, in my like, my third edition of it, it was really, I mean, I wrote something that wasn't, I mean I wrote myself into the story, and I'm like, wait a second, that can't happen. (Interview, 5-29-90)

Unfortunately, the interviewer did not pursue the problem James raised here. But James seems to have been worried about violating the convention Britton discusses above: Authors of fiction objectify their experiences and thoughts in indirect ways that do not speak directly to their audiences. James said, "I wrote myself into the story," and he did. In the second and third editions of *The Fake Line Leader*, he was a character in a fictitious series of events, along with other characters named after children in the classroom. What is most interesting to me is what James could have meant when he said, "that can't happen." Obviously, it did happen so he was not saying it was an impossibility. He seems to have had a sense for the conventional disjunction in fiction between author and personal experiences and values, and was concerned that writing himself "into the story" would in some way violate this convention. Why would he be concerned about this? Was it simply that he did not want to be unconventional in his writing, or, was he perhaps concerned that James, the character, would be perceived as a rather direct representation and expression of James, the third grader? In other words, would writing himself into the story be similar to writing personal narratives, with its risk of self-exposure?

In any event, James and other children wrote predominantly fiction, and, apparently they were not alone in their preference for fiction over writing that was more directly revealing. Barnes and Barnes (1984), in their study of English classes in British secondary schools, found that many students responded to requests for what they called "personal writing" with fiction. The reasons students gave for avoiding personal writing and embracing fiction were similar to those given by my students. Barnes and Barnes concluded that students used "fiction as a way of dealing with first hand experience, since it freed them from the danger of giving too much away or of adopting an unacceptable persona" (cited in Willinsky, 1990, p. 168). These students, as well as my third grade writers, were aware of, and depended on, the partial disjunction between author and material that fiction provided.

But my students valued fiction for more than its avoidance of identifiably personal material. In fact, the most common responses children gave to questions about why they wrote fiction were similar to the initial ones Emily gave above: Fiction was more exciting and interesting than nonfiction. I will explore these responses in relation to children's control over their writing, and argue that fiction afforded them a degree of control that they did not believe they had in other genres. They used this control to satisfy themselves as writers and to satisfy their audiences. I should note that distance and control are not unrelated. In my discussion of distance above, I emphasized the relation of writer to audience, and argued that fiction distanced authors from audiences in a way that lessened risks of exposure. In what follows, the relation of writer to material is an important aspect of control. With distance from the material, children enjoyed a control over their material that they did not enjoy with material more closely tied to what "really happened" in their lives.

———

SUZANNE: It [Fiction] is, it's more interesting, because some people have boring lives.
INTR: Do they?
SUZANNE: And they don't like, I think fiction is more exciting because you can write about anything you want. (Interview, 5-18-90)

Suzanne suggests several themes that run through children's comments on the relative superiority of fiction over writing about real life. The dominant theme is that fiction is more exciting and interesting than nonfiction. Sometimes, personal narratives were denigrated because the lives themselves were deemed inadequate as material—people have boring lives. William said that "nothing really happened" that was worth writing about (Interview, 5-18-90). Other times, the inadequacy seemed to result from children's not being able to identify things worth writing about from their own histories. There were probably things that would be good to write about, but as Ken said, "it's pretty hard to remember. . . . I couldn't think of anything to write about myself" (Interview, 5-31-90). I am reminded here of Dewey's comment that there is all the difference in the world between having something to say and having to say something. Children had to say something, and it might have been easier to move to fiction than to find something in their pasts or presents to write about.

But the adequacy of lives or memories cannot be divorced from children's sense of what their peer audiences might want or enjoy to read. As I noted above, a consistent response to interview questions about why children wrote fiction was that fiction was more exciting and interesting. Below, I discuss this response as a positive affirmation of fiction by young writers, because it was more enjoyable for them to write than nonfiction. But this response has something of a defensive posture in it as well; that is, real life was not interesting *enough* for peer audiences who would be reading and responding to those texts. There is a sense of this posture in Emily's comments that introduced the chapter—she talked about spicing up personal narratives to make them more interesting to read. Part of the risk of writing about themselves was that their lives would not be interesting enough for peers. In their conferences with me, Ken, James, and other children often told me stories that I thought would be great to write down, and I told them so. But children often did not write them down, and if they did, they usually did not publish or share them.

Another theme that ran through a number of children's interviews was that nonfiction (including personal narratives, but also transactional writing such as reports) was more restrictive than fiction. Part of the restrictive nature of nonfiction for children seemed to come from a perceived restriction of possible material. If you wrote about your own life, they seemed to reason, you were limited to things that had happened to you and to things you knew. In other words, you had to use your memory instead of your imagination. John thought that, in contrast to nonfiction, "you have a lot of ideas with fiction . . . you can have more creations" (Interview, 5-21-90). A related reason children thought that nonfiction was restrictive was because children saw it as demanding a fidelity to the truth and to what really happened in a way that fiction obviously did not. They expressed a rather severe referentialist stance to the relation of language to the world in nonfiction, in which the words used had to match up fairly directly with what had really happened. I had the sense, from their interviews, that my students might very well believe that there would only be one correct way to tell a personal narrative, and that the challenge of telling such a story was to get it right. John, for example, asserted that "with nonfiction you've got to be stricter with things that happened." Marie said that she did not really like writing "real stories": "Because, um, if I'm writing something that happened a long time ago, I could be close to the, like in the middle, and then I could forget something and that could ruin the story" (Interview, 5-16-90). Sharon stated that

> It's funner to make, um, things that aren't true because it, you *can do anything you want if things are not true.* If they are true, then you have to make it *really true.* (Interview, 5-30-90; my emphasis)

Children felt they could manipulate their material, that they were in control, when they wrote fiction: But some felt that the material controlled them when they wrote (if they wrote) nonfiction. They seemed to have little sense that they could shape personal narratives or expository topics to different ends, or that the "same story" could be told many different ways.

I am struck here by the resonances between my students' self-descriptions of what it felt like to write nonfiction, and the way that Calkins (1986) described third grade authors writing personal narratives. Calkins observed that third grade writers seemed unable to jump out of any chain of events they happened to be describing: "They rarely interrupted themselves to reflect on their subject or their text . . . or to consider alternative paths . . . writing was a continual process of adding on" (p. 86). Calkins explained these observations with reference to cognitive psychology (specifically, Bereiter & Scardamalia, 1982), and argued that third graders seemed to lack a "'central executive function' that would allow them to shift attention back and forth between reading, writing, talking, thinking, writing, and so forth" (p. 86). I cannot help wondering if what Calkins observed was at least partly a function of the genre and material her third grade research subjects were pursuing—personal narratives. Perhaps these students were just trying to tell the truth, enacting a sort of intuitive philosophical stance on the relation of language to the world, and in so doing, they were restricted by their material and task in ways that did not allow them to be more flexible. Would Calkins have observed the same "continual process of adding on" and moved to the same inference of limited mental functioning if she had watched children writing fiction?

Children at least *felt* in control when writing fiction. They consistently noted that they could "write anything" they wanted, could do anything they wanted in their fiction. And this sense of control seemed to give them pleasure. There were numerous comments that fiction was more exciting and interesting than nonfiction. Both James and Sharon, in their interviews, said that it was "funner" to write fiction than nonfiction; David and Leon used the word "enjoy" when talking about why they wrote fiction. When asked why so many people in the room wrote fiction, Robert replied, "Well, maybe they just wanted to have fun with what they wrote" (Interview, 5-29-90).

Britton (1982) suggests one source of pleasure for children writing fiction that seems in tune with the sense of control my students valued:

> It has often been pointed out that in one sense a tiny infant is lord of his universe, and that growing from infancy into childhood involves discovering one's own unimportance. But the world created in the stories children write is a world they control and this may be a source of deep satisfaction. (p. 165)

When we, and children, tell stories, we are taking on a "spectator role" (Britton, 1978; 1982), an evaluative stance (Bakhtin, 1986), in relation to our own, others, and imagined experience. In stories, we evaluate that experience according to our interests and values, and express those interests and values in the stories we tell—in the objects and events we focus on (and ignore), in the stance we take in relation to those objects and events. With stories, we attempt to make sense of our experience in the world.

The human capacity to tell stories is one way men and women collectively build a significant and orderly world around themselves. With fiction, we investigate, perhaps invent, the meaning of human life. (Miller, 1990, p. 69)

At least part of the pleasure my students took in writing fiction was related to the chance to "build their own worlds," to say for themselves, in stories, what the world is like and/or what the world should be like. Fiction allowed children to express personal visions of the world and their places in it.

Sometimes the worlds children created in their stories were very similar to the worlds they lived in and experienced. Marie's *The Cloud That Smiled*, for example, described the everyday life of its main character (not a cloud) in some detail, and this everyday life had a strong basis in Marie's own experiences. As in some of James and his friends' texts that I discussed earlier, Marie named several of her characters after children in the classroom. In fact, along with Carol, Marie herself appears in the story as a secondary character and friend to the main character, Lisa (who, if you remember, also appeared in *The Fake Line Leader*). In her interview, Marie said that she liked to work with Lisa during the writing workshop, and that Lisa was one of her friends. In addition to appearing in Marie's story as a character, Lisa had another role in this story—she drew the illustrations for the final published version of Marie's book. Through Lisa, as a character, and with her as an illustrator, Marie looked at and evaluated the world around her.

The Cloud that Smiled

Once there was a girl named Lisa. She was 8 years old. Something strange was going on that day because nobody would smile or talk to her. She would smile at them but they just wouldn't smile at her. So that day she went to the playground. She sat on the twirly-slide steps thinking about why people won't smile at her or talk to her. She looked up and thought she saw a cloud smiling! She was amazed.

Then her mother called her and she ran to her mother. She looked up again. She didn't see anything but a cloudy sky. Then her alarm clock went off, then she woke up.

Getting Dressed

But once she woke up she remembered it was Saturday. She was relieved. She looked at the clock—it was 11:00! She quickly got out of bed. Then she went downstairs to eat breakfast. No one was down there, so she figured that they were still sleeping. But it was 11:00. Oh! She heard a noise outside. "What if it's Freddy Krueger?" she thought, but she looked anyway. "Thank heavens!" she said. Her parents, her little brother, and her dog were out there having a snowball fight.

Then she went to the table so she could make herself some Cheerios. So she made herself some Cheerios. After that she went upstairs to get dressed. She was going to wear her jeans and her smiling face shirt. So she got her jeans and she got her smiling face shirt. Except when she got her smiling face shirt it was frowning. "Am I missing something?" she thought. "This better not be a joke."

So she put on her smiling—or frowning shirt and her jeans. After that she went outside. Carol and Marie were playing in Marie's backyard. She asked them if she could play with them. They said no. And after that they said, "Get out of here."

"What's wrong with them?" she thought.

So she went back inside. Then she sat down. She turned on TV. Ninja Turtles were on. She didn't want to watch that. She looked out the window. She couldn't believe her eyes. She saw a cloud smiling! Just like in her dream! Her parents, her brother and her dog interrupted her as they came in. "Who won?" she asked.

They giggled. Then finally her dad said, "The dog did." She started to giggle too. Then she remembered tomorrow was Christmas Eve.

"Mom!" she yelled. "Can I wrap presents?"

"Sure!" she yelled back.She wrapped the present that she got her little brother. She got him a remote control car. By the time she finished wrapping presents, which took her 4 hours, it was 8 o'clock pm, time to have a bedtime snack. After she finished her bedtime snack she went to bed.

The Next Day, At Night

Finally it was Christmas Eve night. It was dinner time. They were having Chinese, her favorite. Once she was finished with dinner, they went out looking at Christmas lights. When they got back it was time for Lisa and her brother Phil to go to bed.

RINGGGGGGGG!

Her alarm clock went off. She jumped out of bed and ran downstairs. She looked at the presents—there were a lot of them. She opened most of them. Finally she got her last one. She opened the present. It was a crystal and a smiling face was carved in it. Her mom said, "How do you like it?"

The End!

In her story, Marie drew on and responded to objects, people, and events from her own experience: the twirly-slide steps on the playground behind Clifford School, Carol and Lisa and her family, Cheerios, figures from popular culture (Freddy Krueger, Teenage Mutant Ninja Turtles), school ("it was Saturday. She was relieved"), traditions surrounding Christmas. One of the reasons I find Marie's story so attractive, I think, is exactly because she created a believable world with her details of and observations on the experiences of an 8-year-old girl. This believable world was the counterpoint to the world of dreams she began with, and then sustained with inversions (friends that would not talk or play with her, a shirt with a smile turned upside-down), and repetitions of the dream world in real life (a smiling cloud, a crystal with a smiling face).

My sense that the world Marie created in her story was closely modeled after her own is strengthened by my knowledge of the rough draft of her story. In the rough draft, Marie had used third person consistently, until the beginning of the second section entitled, "Getting Dressed." From there on, she wrote in first person. In fact, the main character of the story shifted in this section from Lisa to Marie herself:

> So I put on my smiling—or frowning shirt and my jeans. After that I went outside. Carol and Lisa were playing in Lisa's backyard. I asked them if I could play with them. (Rough draft, "The Cloud")

When I pointed this out to Marie, she said that she wanted Lisa to be the main character throughout, and she edited her draft.

Marie's story told a very "personal" narrative, even though it was done in third person and contained improbable elements. In a fictional narrative, she named and evaluated important aspects of her experience. The story world she created strongly resembled the world she experienced each day.

Many children, however, used fiction to create imaginary worlds and play with magic, horror, even, in John's case, time. Of all the children in the room, John pursued some of the most intriguing themes—his *The Second Stories Club* is an excellent example. From the title, you might expect a story about a group of children who meet in the second story of a building, or something like that (there was a movie about teenagers called *The Breakfast Club*). Actually, John's book was a collection of five short narratives. The five narratives shared a common theme: a specific duration of time—the second. Thus, his book was a collection (the *Club* of the title, I think) of narratives (*Stories*) about a duration of time (*The Second*): *The Second Stories Club*.

In the final version of his book, each of the five narratives was followed by an interpretation of that narrative, written by John. When John first wrote his rough draft, I was already aware that his classmates often complained to him that they did not understand his writing. In a writing conference, I suggested that John accompany each of his narratives with a brief discussion of the joke or trick he was playing with that story. I told him that his stories reminded me of abstract paintings, and that artists sometimes included written material with their paintings that discussed what they were attempting to do on canvas (and that some artists considered this written material part of the art work itself). From this discussion, we decided he would write accompanying material for his narratives, and call these discussions "interpretations." As you will see, John could not resist being playful even in his interpretations.

The Second Stories Club

1. Rosie's Long School Holdup

One day Rosie's mom said, "It takes longer time to get there than you'll be there." So, it took a year to get there 'cause of the swirling road. They were there for one second. So Rosie's mom didn't see her for two years and one second

1. Interpretation

Why doesn't Rosie take a short cut! It would only be one year and one second until Rosie's mom saw her.

2. The Very Short Lesson

"Oh silly," said Tom's father. "You won't take lessons from Ai Sekind."
"I don't follow directions."
So the next day he took lessons from Ai Sekind. It was like here, snap, go ahead.

2. Interpretation

The "from" acts like a "for" in "The Very Short Lesson." "Ai Sekind" acts like "a second."

3. A Lot in a Second

One day a baby scribbled all over everywhere. Two judges erased and the dumb, idiotic baby scribbled all over the judges and he ended up as a naughty 6 year old. Even though that was a lot in a second, he ended up in the juvenile home.

3. Interpretation

You know the secrets: a baby cannot hold a marker without getting very messy. And, it would be impossible to scribble that much in a second.

4. The One-Second-Year Old

"Oh no. I'm pregnant. I'm having a baby boy." So eight and a half months went by and he was born. One second after someone else was born. He was a one second year old.

4. Interpretation

It is funny to think of a one second year old.

5. A Long Time to Wait

"Well, this is a long time to wait."
"A second?"
"No. A day."
"A day and a second?"
"No. A day."
"You've got to have some second doing."
"O.K. 1 day and 59 seconds."

5. Interpretation

The guy said, "some second doing." So that's why he did one day and 59 seconds.

John drew on aspects of his experience in his narratives. For example, school and music lessons (John was a serious piano student) figure in his first two stories. He played off a fairly common expression in #1 with his "It takes longer time to get there than you'll be there," which he pushes to an extreme. He told me in one of our writing conferences that he thought that "Ai Sekind" (#2) looked like Arabic names he had seen. And the inspiration for #3, I think, was a story I had told to the class about my (then) 1-year-old son, John Jacob. One morning before school, I had left John Jacob drawing pictures in the middle of the living room with washable magic markers, while I took a shower. When I got out of the shower, I found he had filled a portion of our hallway wall, approximately three feet high (his reach) by six feet wide, with broad, graceful lines in black, not-so-washable (we found out) marker. My third grade John draws the moral for me in his interpretation for #3: A baby cannot hold a marker without getting very messy. And I, too, thought it impossible that my son could "scribble that much" in the time I was in the shower.

John's interpretation of story #4 seems perfect—it is funny to think of a one second year old. As for #5, even with John's interpretation and several discussions about it, I still have not figured out what he was trying to do.

In other stories, John played with numbers (*The Three Thousand Musketeers*) and with human nature (*The Dog Human*), and wrote of above-ground elevators to Miami and Tampa (*The Elevator*). He inspired a host of haunted house stories by other children in the room before Halloween with his *Haunted Horror*, which, within a larger narrative, told the ghastly story of the newspaper man:

> One day a man sneaked in for a report. He was a newspaper man. He pushed the button, the house laughed, and a bat went out. The cats opened the gates and chased him. A witch answered the door and the vampires got him and he was never seen again.

In his fiction, John could create worlds held together by idiosyncratic interests in time, word play, numbers, Halloween. This was what he valued about fiction—as he said in his interview, "you have a lot of ideas with fiction . . . you can have more creations."

Personal creations. Above I argued that one of a complex of reasons children wrote fiction was because of the disjunction it afforded between author and material. Fictional narratives lessened risks of self-exposure because they were "fake stories," lies. Within them (and behind them) children could explore real and imagined experiences through the creation of characters who might or might not speak for them.

But fiction also afforded children control over their material, a control they appropriated more and less effectively to express their individ-

ual interests and values. They could do "what they wanted to" in their
writing within constraints set by, among other things, the perceived
expectations of peer audiences for interesting, exciting stories. Thus, fictional narratives could also be very personal narratives, offering, in the
selection and affirmation of this and not that, an expression of the
writer's vision, her thoughts and desires.

Children knew and depended on the distance fiction provided to
avoid self-exposure. At the same time, they also knew that they were
exposed in their fiction, that they put themselves at risk in the telling of
even acceptable lies. The words of children I quoted above—speaking of
trusted and untrusted audiences, how it felt to be teased about stories—
came from children who wrote primarily fiction. Karen stopped reading
a fictionalized account of Mrs. Parker's childhood, not her own childhood, when Ken joined us out in the hall. John ended up in the principal's office for reading and defending a story he wrote about an imaginary elevator that transported people to Florida. Jessie would not share
her retelling of "Sleeping Beauty," despite my efforts to create a classroom in which young authors trusted their audiences.

> Once upon a time there was a beautiful princess, and her name was
> Jessie. One day, she was sleeping, and she heard a noise so she got up
> and went upstairs to the room upstairs. When she opened the door she
> saw a spinning wheel.
>   When she was spinning at the spinning wheel, she poked her finger.
> Suddenly she fell asleep, and everyone fell asleep too. Just then a
> prince came.
>   He snuck into the castle and found the princess and kissed her. And
> suddenly everybody awoke and the prince became an empire.

Bruner (1990) believes that the stories we tell and write "mediate
between the canonical world of culture and the more idiosyncratic world
of beliefs, desires, and hopes" (p. 52). If I understand him correctly,
Bruner is saying that our stories represent a sort of compromise between
how we think the world *is* (given to us in the "canonical world of culture") and how we, as individuals, would like the world to be. When we
tell stories, we both draw on given, cultural narratives about the world
and our place in it, and manipulate and twist them in ways that express
our "idiosyncratic worlds." The twists Jessie gave to a more canonical
version of "Sleeping Beauty" (from the Grimms, for example), are charming, and suggest self-importance, youth, movement. Her princess is
named Jessie, instead of Rosamond. Jessie, the author (as well as Jessie
the princess), avoids altogether the angry witch who casts a death spell
on the young princess, and the good witch who transmutes that spell to

sleep. Jessie seems impatient with sleep, so she has her princess "suddenly" fall asleep, only to be awakened almost immediately by a prince who "just then" arrived. In the Grimm version, the two live happily ever after together. Jessie's princess and prince may do likewise, but Jessie leaves this open. Jessie, however, is not content with some sort of romantic bliss for the two. Her version ends with the rise to power of her prince: He became an empire.

Jessie's story may also be read against another "canonical world of culture"—the peer culture in which Jessie participated. The rift between canonical peer world and Jessie's more idiosyncratic one is wide, and leaves the peer one looking anything but charming (a little grim), for Jessie. In that culture, Jessie was not beautiful in the stories others told about her. She labored to avoid those who would cast spells to "cut her in half" or turn her into a "jar of slime." The school year was long, and she had little chance of association (nor did she say she wanted it) with the powerful.

Writing felt risky for children in the writing workshop, and it seemed riskier to some than others. Children responded by seeking out trusted audiences, be they peers or teachers, and by turning, often, to fiction, writing themselves onto the page from a slight distance.

Jessie wrote herself and a vision of the world on the page, sometimes through personal narrative, other times through fiction. But others seldom heard her voice or saw her vision, at least not in the public spaces the workshop provided. Jessie thought that those spaces were for people with "lots of friends."

———

Jessie did not assert herself, with her texts, in the public spaces of sharing time and the writing workshop library. Other children toward the bottom of the informal peer hierarchies, however, did. Janis and John were among the most frequent readers during sharing time. William had two books in the library, and Jil's story, *Kittens*, and Janis's book of riddles and jokes, *The Funny Book*, were among the more popular, and most checked out, books in the workshop library.

But there was an interesting, and ultimately disturbing, difference between the public texts of these children and the texts written by children with more status and power in the room. Children with little status tended not to write themselves or their friends into their stories as characters. Children with more status did. The result was that only certain children regularly appeared in the stories read by children during sharing time and housed in the workshop library—children with the most status and power in the room.

The contrast can be sharply represented with the opening pages from books written by children toward the bottom and the top of the informal pecking order in the room. The first two pages of William's book, *The Junkie House* ("junkie" from "junk," not a reference, at least not a direct one, to drug users), are reproduced in Figure 5.2. The opening page of Carol's book, *Spies*, appears in Figure 5.3.

William does not name the main character in his story after himself or anyone else in the room—in fact, in this instance William's main character is referred to only as "a person," "the person," and "he" throughout the story. In Carol's story, the main characters are named for children in the room; specifically, a group of four girls of relatively high status, including Carol herself. Three of the children's names are shortened and stylized, with the effect, for me, of suggesting characters who are tougher or more sophisticated than characters named by the full names: Car (from Carol), 'Zanne (from Suzanne), and Lis (from Lisa). (Several children in interviews mentioned that high status boys and girls in the room had better clothes than other children. The attention to clothes and hair in Carol's illustration is striking, especially in contrast to William's illustration.)

The situation, of course, was more complex than is suggested by the juxtaposition of William and Carol's stories, in at least three ways. First, children of relatively high status and influence in the room did not always

There were two black dogs and two black cats. They lived in a junkie house.

One day a person opened the door and stepped into the house. And the cat jumped on him. The person threw the cat.

Figure 5.2. From William's *The Junkie House.*

write stories that included themselves and their friends as characters. Troy, for example, who worked with James on one of the *Fake Line Leader* sequels, wrote an extremely popular book entitled, *The Magic Triceratops*. Its main characters were a dinosaur and a boy named Chang; none of the characters in the story were named explicitly for children in the room.

Second, children with little status did occasionally write themselves and/or friends into their stories. However, as with Jessie, most of these stories did not go public. Robert, for example, wrote a fictional narrative about adventures that he and his cousin had on Halloween. Robert had his text typed and bound, and he drew illustrations for the book. But he never shared it in sharing time or put it in the classroom library. He did publish a story about pirates and skeletons, in which the characters were named just that—Pirates and Skeletons.

John, however, did write and share some stories that at least seemed to place him as a main character in his own fictional narratives. I say "seemed" because, unlike stories by James and Carol, John's stories never explicitly named him as a character in his stories. He often wrote in first person, leaving it unclear as to whom the "I" referred: the author, or a persona created by him. For example, John's *The Elevator* began:

**It was time for the club.
"Come on," said 'Zanne. So they
went to the door that led them to
the laboratory under the ground.**

Figure 5.3. From Carol's Spies.

> One day me, Jimmy, and our two American Saddle horses, Joe and
> Jack, started a club. We had a secret clubroom, and we two lived there
> except when visiting our parents.

As in Carol's story, *Spies*, the characters in John's story belong to a club,
have an underground meeting place, and are soon engaged in an adventure. Unlike Carol's story, none of the characters (not even the horses)
are explicitly named for children in the room. John and his friends in
class, in other words, were not present in his stories in the same way that
James and Carol and their friends were.

   Of relatively low status children, only Jil seems to have named herself as a character in a public text (I assert this after a close examination
of the books that appeared in the workshop library and after a less sys-
tematic perusal of fieldnotes and audiotapes pertaining to sharing time
across the year). In her book, *Kittens,* Jil wrote in the first person, and
does not identify the "I" of the story as "Jil" anywhere in her text. But she
does name the main character "Jil" in an illustration on page eight of her
fourteen page book (see Figure 5.4).

   Finally, we must remember that simply being included (or present)
as a character in a story is not necessarily a positive thing. In chapter 3,
I discussed several texts in which characters named for children in the
room were portrayed negatively by James and his friends, and I noted
Sharon and Carol's sentiments about being included in texts written by
boys. The point here (as well as the thrust of this discussion) is perhaps
most starkly illustrated with the list of characters Mary and Suzanne drew
up for a play they had written. In the column to the left are the characters' names in Mary and Suzanne's play. To the right are the names of
children Mary and Suzanne thought should play those parts. Except for
Joshua, who was Suzanne's fifth grade neighbor, all the children listed
were from the classroom.

Mouse	Maya
Princess	Marie
Stranger	Ken
King	Paul
Prince	Troy
Witch	Lori
Queen	Carol
Tower 1	John
Tower 2	Leon
Tower 3	Robert
Dancers	Suzanne and Joshua
Narrator	Bruce

Figure 5.4. From Jil's Kittens.

Not all characters in plays are created equal. Three characters (and only these characters) had no lines in the play: Tower 1, Tower 2, and Tower 3. These roles were assigned, by Mary and Suzanne, to John, Leon, and Robert, three boys at the bottom of the pecking order. Leon and Robert lived in the trailer park, and John, as has already been discussed, was often teased by his classmates. They were to stand on the stage from the beginning to the end of the play, present throughout, but mute.

———

So where does this leave us? In general, children of high status and influence in the room appeared as characters in the public stories of the writing workshop; other children did not. When these other children did appear, their inclusion did not necessarily suggest positive regard. *Certain children were privileged in the content of the public texts of the work-*

shop. The micropolitics of peer relations played itself out not only on the playground and behind my back, but in the writing children chose to make public in the spaces created and authorized by me, the teacher.

It is disturbing enough to realize that children's texts might reflect, in some way, differences in status and power among children. But we must also consider the active role these texts might play in maintaining these relationships. Texts are rhetorical; they can influence how people think, have effects in the world. When a child is not chosen to play baseball by her classmates during recess, this not only reflects their evaluations of her as a player or friend in some passive way, it also actively produces (and reproduces) those evaluations for the child and her classmates. The classmates' decisions have effects, make a difference for the future, maybe make recess less joyful, and the child more anxious and clumsy the next day when she is picked to play, and evaluated again.

On some level, children knew this about their texts, knew they were rhetorical. It took longer for me to understand. Witness Lisa during sharing time, in November, as she introduces her "soap opera" in which all the main characters are children from the class; note my response that pursues socioanalysis and abstracted relations among women and men, and ignores the immediate relations of children in the room:

> Sharing time: Grace gave a little speech about what kind of behavior we expected, and then Lisa shared her piece. I thought it was interesting that Lisa, before reading, said the piece was about people in the class, and that if anyone wasn't in her piece yet, they probably would be later. What does this mean? Is she recognizing the importance of being included in these stories for feelings and status?
>
> She read quickly, and students and Grace asked her to read more slowly (Jil told her if she felt "hyper" she should still slow down the next time she read her piece). Suzanne said that she thought the piece was "excellent" (quite a contrast here to how she opened her response to Emily the other day—social class, status stuff going on?), but that she didn't understand the part where the characters of Jessie and Paul were talking about "caring." Suzanne asked, "Caring about what?"
>
> In the story, the character of Jessie says to Paul, "I didn't know you cared," and Paul says, "I don't." When Lisa repeated this part of the story, Robert started razzing the real life Paul, pushed his shoulders. Paul looked down, seemed embarrassed, but was smiling. Somewhere in here Grace said, "Soap operas come to Mrs. P's class," or something like that. And she was right. Given this, some sort of examination of what female and male characters are doing in Lisa's story, and maybe a discussion of this with her and the class, might be important (look at anti-sexist pedagogy material). I could do this with Lisa when she is revising. If women and men take on stereotyped roles, we could play with reversing roles and see what happened. Another issue here, of course, is that Lisa has been working on this piece a long time, and I don't want to discourage her. (Fieldnotes, 11-20-89)

I was beginning to wonder about peer relations among children here, but primarily in relation, not to written texts, but to their talk and behavior in class (as when I questioned Suzanne's motivations for responding positively to Lisa, and negatively to Emily). Lisa raised the issue of the inclusion and exclusion of children in stories explicitly, but I did not develop it here. And at this point in my teaching and research, I do not appear to be very sensitive to the embarrassment and hurt Jessie and Paul might have experienced from Lisa's textual teasing, and the ensuing discussion of it. Particularly Jessie: In Lisa's soap opera, Jessie assumed (and seemed to desire) a romantic relationship with a boy, assumed wrong, and was put down (Jessie: I didn't know you cared; Paul: I don't). It seems I reported this episode in my fieldnotes only to set up Grace's characterization of Lisa's story as a soap opera, which sets up the need for a little socioanalysis. I considered problems Lisa's material posed for my response to her, but I did not consider problems Lisa's material posed for other children in the room.

I do not know why John, Janis, William, Karen, and others, did not publish fictional narratives like Lisa's, with themselves and classmates as characters in the story. If they had reasons they could articulate, I did not ask for them. I discovered this aspect of their texts long after I was done teaching. My first guess would be that risks these children associated with writing about themselves in personal narratives also attended writing themselves into fictional narratives, and that they judged these risks prohibitive. In this interpretation, children of low status were less extreme versions of Jessie, but living with similar concerns. They did not remove themselves and their texts from the public spaces of sharing time and the library, as Jessie did, but they did remove their names. The conventional disjunction between author and material in fiction was not quite enough to make them feel comfortable putting themselves back into their texts as characters. This would not explain all their decisions. Sometimes, perhaps many times, they simply were interested in writing about other characters in other stories: Mrs. Parker as a little girl with a dog and a boyfriend; music lessons from (for) Ai Sekind (a second). Children with more status and influence, from this view, felt less vulnerable. They wrote fiction, but were more comfortable with placing themselves in their stories.

Or, perhaps, the children at the top were also uncomfortable in the workshop, but for different reasons. Sharing time and the library offered less popular children in the room numerous public opportunities to impress peers and teachers with their wit, to influence opinion on what *really* was scary about Halloween. Unlike the playground or the cafeteria, or before and after school, these public spaces were somewhat closely watched over by teachers who would not allow these other children to be shouted down or pushed around. Perhaps the pecking order was a little more up for grabs than I have suggested, and the workshop was an open but structured place in which there was

> An exchange of evaluations between authors and their readers, an exchange in which reputations are made and lost, influences wax and wane, values gain and lose currency, and the cultural pattern of a social group is sustained and evolved. (Britton, 1978, p. 17)

Children at the top wrote themselves into their texts as an assertion (and reassertion) of their importance, their rightful place at the front of the room and at the focus of attention. From this perspective, they named themselves in their texts in the name of order, in defense of hierarchies that were continually threatened by upstart writers like Jil, John, and Janis. Remember James' comments, in chapter 3, about Leon trying to be someone he was not, not staying in his place.

> A story is a way of doing things with words. It makes something happen in the real world: for example, it can propose modes of self-hood or ways of behaving that are then imitated in the real world. It has been said, along these lines, that we would not know we were in love if we had not read novels. Seen from this point of view, fictions may be said to have a tremendous importance not as the accurate reflectors of a culture but as the makers of that culture and as the unostentatious, but therefore all the more effective, policemen of culture. Fictions keep us in line and tend to make us more like our neighbors. (Miller, 1990, p. 69)

It would be difficult to characterize all the "lines" that fictions in the workshop would keep children within. The texts shared by children from the author's chair and in the workshop library pursued multiple interests and values. Most children, regardless of their place in peer hierarchies, contributed to the collections of public texts in the room. They chose material that they more or less effectively bent to their wills, and they shared those texts with others.

Still, in their inclusions and exclusions, in their evaluations, these texts valued certain children more than others. And the children receiving valorization on the page were children who did not live in the trailer park, were children who already enjoyed status and influence within the peer culture, even if they had to work to keep it.

In my thinking about teacher response to children's texts, I had realized that children in writing workshops made important curricular decisions for themselves, and that some of the material they might work with required critical evaluations by them with my help. But I had thought of children's decisions about material as private ones, affecting only individual children's work for the duration of individual projects. I had not considered how children's stories became curriculum for other children in teacher-sponsored events and classroom institutions that encouraged (and required) children to listen to and read carefully the texts of other children. I had thought of "questionable" material in children's texts as the unfortunate traces of societal politics of class, race, and gender. I had not considered how children's stories might participate, for better and for worse, in the micropolitics of the classroom.

But I would learn.

Chapter **6**

Teacher Response to Children's Texts

When my younger daughter made disparaging remarks about Billy Budd I rushed to Melville's defense with a speech on the conflict between the rule of law applied generically and the merits of individual cases. Billy Budd struck a superior officer, I reminded her; according to the letter of the law, he must hang. And yet, and yet, we cannot quite swallow it. . . . I ended in a glow of ambivalence. "It wasn't that he struck him," she murmured. "He killed him."

Lynne Sharon Schwartz
True Confessions of a Reader

The last three chapters have been true confessions of a reader. I read the nonverbal, oral, and written texts of third graders in my writing workshop, and told stories about student intention, the risks, for children, of writing , the lure of fiction. I warmed myself a little (and you, I hope) in the glow of ambivalence, that pleasure we get from playing with complexity and contradiction when we do not have to decide what is to be done with Billy Budd, or James, or Jessie. Lynne Sharon Schwartz's younger daughter murmurs in this chapter. Here are the confessions of a teacher struggling with complexity and contradiction, warmed by nervousness, frustration, and the heat of confrontation between actual people, not just the clash of meanings and interpretations.

Maya's text, *The Zit Fit: The Lovers in the School*, provoked oral responses to Maya on two successive days, and five pages of written notes on the night in between—five pages written after I seemed to be wrapping up my notewriting with this comment: "I'm running out of gas very quickly (it's after midnight). Some brief comments on Maya's text" (Fieldnotes, 3-8-90). The comments were not brief. As I read Maya's story and wrote and thought about the problems and issues I had to confront,

I worried more and more about what a responsible sort of response would look like in this situation.

In what follows, I offer a story and an interpretation of my oral and written responses to Maya and her text. Interpretation, as Scholes (1985) reminds us, "depends upon the failures of reading. It is the feeling of incompleteness on the reader's part that activates the interpretive process" (p. 22). In this case, it is the two conceptions of teacher response to children's texts that I brought to this work (discussed in chapter 1) that lead to "failures of reading." Both following the child and response as socioanalysis, as conceptions of teacher response to children's texts, proved inadequate for reading (making sense of) what happened and what was at stake. As I tell the story of my response to Maya's text, I also begin a critique of these conceptions of response that I continue in the final chapter.

My story begins at least a month before I saw Maya's *The Zit Fit*, with a flurry of oral and written texts involving and surrounding Jessie. Some of these texts taught me about the word "zits" (slang for pimples) and the local uses it was put to by these third graders. Other texts suggested a possible friendship, or at least some connection, between Jessie and Jil that I had not picked up on in the classroom, and that would become important for my later response to Maya's story.

On a Wednesday morning in early February, I got to school before the children were allowed into the school building. Groups of children often met me as I walked from the parking lot to say hello, tease me—"Hello Mr. Lens-crafter" (the eyeglass specialists) was an enduring favorite—or, on cold mornings, to complain about having to wait outside. On this day, I saw Suzanne and Robert, among others, yelling at Jessie, calling her "zit face." I told them to stop it, and made a point to walk up to Jessie, touch her on the shoulder, and say good morning. Jessie paused long enough to say hello before continuing her own verbal defense and attack.

These verbal fights continued over the next few days. I wrote in my notes that "Jessie has been doing battle with Mary, Suzanne, Carol, and even sometimes, it seems, her friends Karen and Janis. But primarily with Suzanne and Mary" (Fieldnotes, 2-9-90). Friday, during writing time, I talked with Jessie about a book she had recently published. She refused to share it with any of her classmates.

> I went out into the hall with Jessie, we sat on the floor, and she read her *My Friends* story. She had on outrageous tights (white with big

black polka dots) and a polka dot dress, pink. The day before, she came to school with two piggy tails that stood straight up in the air. She complained about them to me, and dared me to say she didn't look awful. When I said I thought her pigtails looked interesting, she walked away. (Fieldnotes, 2-9-90)

Jessie's book had two chapters. The first chapter was entitled "The Fight," and read:

When Jil and I met each other we fought a lot. But the second day at school we were friends. Then the third day at school we were best friends. On the fourth day we never played with anyone else. We were in kindergarten.

I found another text connecting Jessie and Jil a little later that same day, in the wastebasket (see Figure 6.1). I noticed it when the children left for lunch. In the story, Jil, Jessie, and Paul sing a "dumb" song together before Lisa shoots Jessie in the back. I do not know who the author was, or why he or she threw it away. (It may have been a remnant from Lisa's soap opera, discussed briefly in the last chapter, that I had not seen.)

Actually, I have a guess as to at least one reason it was thrown away. The attack on Jessie was not the only one accomplished with the piece of paper I found in the wastebasket. Below the story reproduced in Figure 6.1 was a message, written in cursive. The message read: "Mary you'r

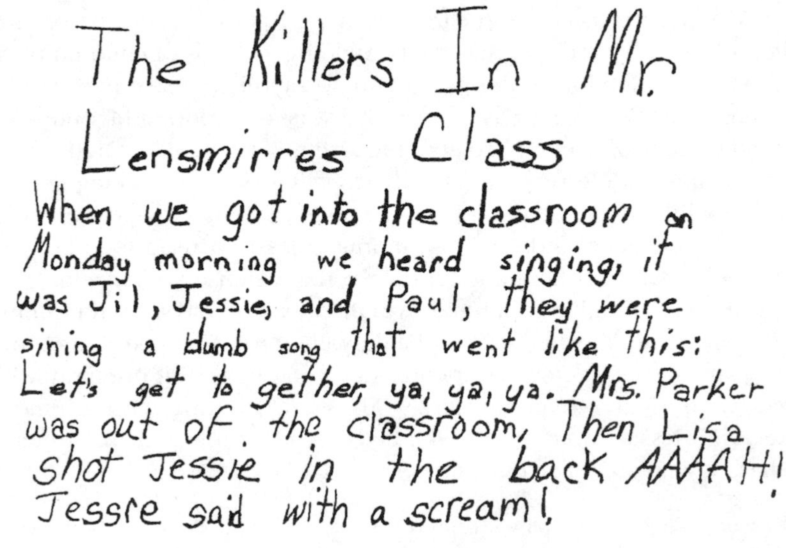

The Killers In Mr. Lensmirres Class
When we got into the classroom on Monday morning we heard singing, it was Jil, Jessie, and Paul, they were sining a dumb song that went like this: Let's get to gether, ya, ya, ya. Mrs. Parker was out of the classroom, Then Lisa shot Jessie in the back AAAAH! Jessie said with a scream!

Figure 6.1. Figure from wastebasket.

stupid!" It was written twice, once in pen and once in pencil. On the back of the paper was: "To: Mary." Maybe the author of "The Killers" ran out of paper, and used the empty space beneath the story for a message, which Mary received and then threw away. Or perhaps the story itself was the first message, and was given to Jessie, Jil, Paul, or maybe even Lisa, by Mary, who then received a critical response to her work—you'r stupid—which she threw away. In any event, the story again associated Jessie with Jil; and Jessie was being attacked in real life and as a fictional character.

When I was writing my notes that night, I remembered that I had run into "zit face" in a writing conference even before I had heard it used orally against Jessie. Suzanne had been writing a rather impressive text inspired by a novel—Margaret Sidney's *Five Little Peppers and How They Grew*—her grandmother had given to her. Suzanne's book was entitled, *The Missing Piece*, and told stories about a family of sisters and brothers and their father—the mother had died. The book had five chapters, and one of them was entitled "Zit Face." This particular chapter involved Kim, her father, her brother Ken, and her older sister Elaine.

> Kim was getting so much zits she did not want to go to school. Nobody liked Kim. Her new name was Zit Face. Her friends said, "Run, run, as fast as you can, you can't catch me you're the Zit man." They called her Zit man because all the boys in 5th grade had Zits. Ken would sing the song on the bus and on the playground and at home. Dad would ground him if he was around when he would sing it by Dad. Dad was very strict. "Run, run, run, as fast as you can, you can't catch me you're the Zit man, Zit, Zit, Zit, man, man, man."
> "Stop it!" outbursted Elaine.

Suzanne seems to have appropriated and transformed (a la Bakhtin) a children's song about a gingerbread man for her own purposes. The song usually goes, "Run, run, as fast as you can, you can't catch me I'm the gingerbread man." The residual influence in the traditional song might account for the shift from "Zit Face" in the title of the chapter and the begining of the story ("Her new name was Zit Face"), to "Zit *man*" in Ken's song—also, "Zit man" completes the rhyme with "can"; "face" would not.

But the song also shows traces of the sort of chasing games and teasing Thorne (1986) described in relation to "female pariahs" in elementary schools. These girls were often called "cootie queens," and cooties, a sort of imaginary social virus, could be spread with physical contact. Chasing games, where the person caught and touched got cooties, and elaborate rules for avoiding and passing on cooties, revolved around these unfortunate girls labeled as "cootie queens." Such games functioned to isolate these girls from other children.

Suzanne's story suggests that "zits" might have served similar functions to "cooties." Ken's song in the story sets up a chase, and expresses the perspective of the one being chased. The song is directed at the Zit man (Kim in Suzanne's story), perhaps called over the shoulder during the chase, and tells her that she can run as fast as she wants, but she will never catch him. The song instructs the one with zits on the futility of trying to make contact with others—they will continue to actively avoid her, try as she might.

Suzanne's use of "zit face" and "zit man" in her written text paralleled oral uses of such words, by her and others, to tease and isolate Jessie before school. Suzanne may have had Jessie in mind when she made up the character of Kim. I found it interesting that, given what I saw of Suzanne's treatment of Jessie in real life, her story included a condemnation of just this sort of teasing by two important characters in her book: the father and Elaine. I had written in my fieldnotes at the time that "while the character [Kim] is cruelly treated in the story, the father does not condone it" (Fieldnotes, 2-9-90).

The father's actions in Suzanne's story were not so surprising—we might expect a young writer to portray a parent as censuring such teasing, even if the child herself did not see any problem with teasing other children. But having Elaine "outburst" "Stop it!" was different. In the other chapters, Elaine is presented by Suzanne as an intelligent, caring older sister. That Suzanne had Elaine object to Ken's teasing suggests an evaluative position, on the author's part, that at least recognized the questionable nature of such teasing and its possible consequences for the person teased. Later, I will argue that Maya took no such evaluative position in *The Zit Fit*, and that this was one of the things that concerned me in my response to it.

I had collected some records of what individual children were working on at different times during the year. In early February, at the same time that Suzanne and Jessie were producing the oral and written texts discussed above, Maya was working on *The Zit Fit: The Lovers in the School*. "Zit face" and "zit man" and "zit fit" were in the air and on the page.

———

Maya had been asking to share the last couple days. She got put off on Wednesday because, with the shortened period, we didn't have any sharing. Today, I intended for her to share, but several obstacles arose. I wanted to conference with her about what she was going to share. The sharing sessions haven't been going well—because of long, boring texts, ineffective reading, the arrangement (kids too far away to see illustrations), maybe kids are alienated from the particular author, busy writing/reading themselves, etc. And Maya has some confusing texts which are hard to follow. Maya couldn't find her text at first—I conferenced with other people, and finally got to Maya a little before sharing time. (Fieldnotes, 3-8-90)

I called Maya over to the round table toward the side of the room. As she sat down, we started talking:

LENSMIRE: Okay, what do you want to share?

MAYA: It's only chapter 1.

LENSMIRE: Okay, what is this zit fit thing, what is this about?

MAYA: Her name is Jil and she loves Jake, okay? You want me to read it to you?

LENSMIRE: Let me read parts and you can explain it to me. (I start reading) "Once there was a girl named Jil. One day she wanted zits to get a boy friend." What does that mean?

MAYA: She wanted zits.

LENSMIRE: And then she could get a boyfriend?

MAYA: Yes. (Long pause, about 8 seconds. I read a few more lines silently)

LENSMIRE: How do you think Jil's going to feel about her name being in it? We should talk to Jil.

MAYA: Oh we told her, we already told her.

LENSMIRE: Let's, let's ask . . . Jil? (Jil walks over to the table) You're in this, or your name is in this zit fit thing. Is that all right with you? If it's not then we'll have to, we'll ask Maya to change the name. Tell you what, Maya—

MAYA: It's not true.

LENSMIRE: Let's do this Maya—

MAYA: I'm not changing—

LENSMIRE: Maya, Maya, this is what we need to do. Uh, let's let Jil read it, okay? Jil doesn't agree to it, you'll have to go back and change the name of it, okay? I'm a little worried because I don't want people's feelings to be hurt by this.

MAYA: Hey, I've already changed James' name.

LENSMIRE: Uh, huh. But we just have to, we just have to be careful, okay? So this is what we're going to do. I'm going to ask Lisa to read her story today and I'm going to write "Friday" here, for Maya. (I write "Friday" in the left margin of Maya's text. In the background, Grace is bringing the writing time segment of the workshop period to a close, and asking the class to get ready for sharing time.) Then, what we're going to do is let Jil read it and then I'm going to read it, and hopefully you'll be able to read it tomorrow in class. Do you have another piece you'd like to read in case this one doesn't come through? (Maya nods) Okay, all right, can you give this to Jil then?

MAYA: Yes. (Audiotape, 3-8-90)

I had not read the entire text. Maya gave it to Jil, who took it back to her seat to read. After sharing time, Jil gave me Maya's story. Jil had written, in the left margin in pencil, "change the name from me to someone else" (see Figure 6.2). That night I read Maya's story through (I have done some editing in the version below):

The Zit Fit: The Lovers in the School

Once there was a girl named Jil. One day she wanted zits to get a boy friend. When Jil went to school there was a new boy. He went to Jil and said, "Would you like some drugs for zits?" Well Jil said, "Sure." The new boy said, "Here's the drugs for zits."

With that going on, another new boy comes to another class. There in the class was Jake Madison, the boy Jil loved and (who) had zits. Then Jil stared and stared until Mrs. Parker said, "Jil, are you all right?"

Jil said, "Hu hu." Everybody started laughing at Jil. She was so embarrassed that she ran out the door screaming to go to her mom. Finally Jil stopped and went back to school. She got in the door about 11:50. That meant it was lunch time. After lunch it was recess. Jake wanted Jil to play with him. Jil knew she could not let Jake down, so Jil went to Jake and Jil said, "Would you like to play with me?"

Jake said, "Sure, if you want."

Jil said, "I didn't have anyone to play with so you were my last hope."

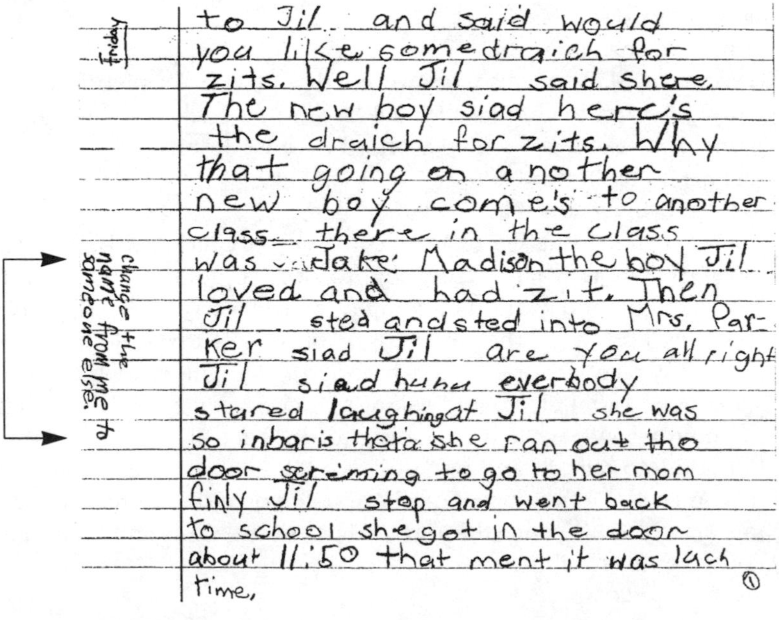
Friday

to Jil and said would
you like somedraich for
zits. Well Jil said shere.
The new boy siad here's
the draich for zits. Why
that going on a nother
new boy come's to another
class. there in the class
was Jake Madison the boy Jil
loved and had zit. Then
Jil sted andsted into Mrs, Parker siad Jil are you all right
Jil siad huhu everbody
stared laughingat Jil she was
so inbaris thata she ran out tho
door scriming to go to her mom
finly Jil stop and went back
to school shegot in the door
about 11:50 that ment it was lach
time,

①

change the name from me to someone else.

Figure 6.2. Jil's marginal comment on Maya's *The Zit Fit.*

> Jake said, "OK, let's go play with the fat boys."
> Jil said, "They always beat me up."
> Jake said, "I'll make sure they won't." Jil could tell Jake loved her.
> When they went to the fat boys they did beat Jil up. Jake scared them away. After that Jake turned around and kissed Jil.

In the conference, I began reading Maya's text as a fictional narrative. There were common markers for the beginning of a story—"Once" and "One day"—and a main character and the problem she faced were established (Jil wanted a boyfriend). I was puzzled, and a little repulsed, by the idea that the character of Jil would want zits, and I asked Maya, "What does this mean?" I was trying to make sense of the fictional world Maya was creating. After she answered with, "She wanted zits," I made a sort of prediction to see if I understood how things worked in this strange place: "And then she could get a boyfriend?"

After Maya answered, there was a pause, and when I began talking with Maya again, my reading of what sort of text this was had shifted from a fictional narrative to a written version of the verbal attacks children subjected each other to on the playground and in the classroom. I now read the text as *an utterance that participated directly in the immediate social relations of real children* in the room. I was worried about people being hurt by this text: "How do you think Jil's going to feel about her name being in it?" Ethical and political issues were at stake: how we would treat each other here; what rights people had to control an important part of their identities—their names; what part texts such as this one played in establishing, maintaining, and changing social relations among children.

Why did my reading of Maya's text shift in the conference? And was the shift justified? I am guessing that during the long pause, I read at least to the line where "Jake Madison" was introduced. Maya had erased, incompletely, the name "James" and written "Jake" over it, leaving "Jake Madison." This did not conceal who she was referring to very effectively, since James Madison was a child in the class, our author of *The Fake Line Leader from Alabama*. This, plus the unusual spelling of "Jil," with Jil in the class spelling her name that way, probably moved me to my second reading. As to whether or not the shift was justified, that was one of the things I tried to figure out in my fieldnotes that night.

Maya never gave any indication that "Jil" did not refer to Jil (Jil is usually spelled with two l's, connecting "Jil" to Jil—of course, a third grader might not have experience with another spelling). In her response, Jil says "change the name from me." Does this mean Jil did read it as a reference to herself, or is it that writing something like "change the character's name of Jil to another name" is more difficult? But both Maya's revision (changing "James" to "Jake") and Jil's use of "me" suggest that Jil and James are in the story. (Fieldnotes, 3-8-90)

I ignored, in the above, a fairly obvious clue that located this story in this classroom—Maya uses the regular classroom teacher's name, Mrs. Parker, in her story.

I also tried to justify my reading of Maya's text as a verbal attack with reference to what I knew about the word "zit," and by contrasting it to Suzanne's chapter, "Zit Face."

> The zit thing is troubling, especially given the import of the word "zit" in the class. It was the word used to ostracize Jessie. And whereas Suzanne pulls it off, Maya doesn't. How doesn't she pull it off? She doesn't recognize and note how hurtful this could be. (Fieldnotes, 3-8-90)

In these notes, I made an explicit connection between Maya's use of the word "zit" and the teasing I had watched Jessie endure. And the texts that I had read (and discussed above), in which Jessie and Jill were connected to each other, strengthened the association I made between what was happening to Jil in Maya's story and what had happened with Jessie.

I also invoked Suzanne's chapter in this note, and attempted to criticize Maya's text through contrast. "This" in the final line of my fieldnotes clearly referred to the use of the word "zits" in Maya's story. Suzanne's story had characters that voiced objections to verbal attacks on another character. She had "pulled off" telling a story about children teasing one another using the word "zits," without making their behavior seem entirely acceptable. That seems to be what I was concerned with here. Maya, however, apparently does not pull this off, because she "doesn't recognize and note how hurtful this [using 'zits'] could be."

But this evaluation missed the way Maya's text worked. Suzanne could have characters tease and object to teasing—could "recognize and note how hurtful this could be"—because these things happened within the fictional world she had created. Maya's text was different. Verbal attacks using the word "zits" do not occur within the fictional world Maya created (although other sorts of attacks did—I address this later). In fact, one of the things that bothered me right at the beginning of our conference was the seeming positive evaluation of zits by the characters of Jil and James. Maya said that Jil *wanted* zits so she could get a boyfriend. Consequently, it makes little sense to demand that Maya somehow object, in her story, to teasing involving "zits," since that does not occur there.

What I interpreted as a verbal attack on Jil was not accomplished by having one character in the story call another character "zit face" or "zit man" (as had happened in Suzanne's story). Instead, the attack depended on attributing to Jil (and James) a desire for something most people seek to avoid: zits. I may have been more repulsed by this attribution to Jil than third graders would be. That is, I might bring meanings to "zits" as an adult—adolescent memories of pimples that sprouted before important dates, or the association of acne with infection—that younger children would not bring. Still, the uses of "zits" by third graders for exclusion and hurting others made it a potent word, and one I doubted Jil or James would want to be associated with.

In the first moments of our writing conference, I shifted from reading Maya's text as a fictional narrative to reading it as a verbal attack on children in the room. My response assumed that the text would be read by children in the class as involving actual children—Jil and James. With this assumption, my response became caught up in a fairly direct way with social relations, norms, and the sharing of texts within the writing workshop.

One of the reasons Maya's story disturbed me was because I associated it with the verbal attacks I saw Jessie encounter. Jessie was not a passive victim, nor did she think of herself in those terms, but she often fought back alone against groups of children. Jil was also often alone in the workshop, although not as unpopular as Jessie. My sense of who the underdogs were among the children, and wanting to insert myself in these relations of power for their benefit, influenced my response. My sense of such things, of course, could have been wrong.

Carol, on several occasions and in relation to Maya's story, told me just that—that I was wrong. It turned out that Carol was something of a secret collaborator with Maya on this text, probably the other of the "we" Maya referred to in our writing conference when she said, "Oh we told her, we already told [Jil]" about the story. When Carol found out later that I wanted Maya to change the character's name from Jil to something else, she told me that Jil just had us teachers fooled, that she was "not such a nice person at all" (Fieldnotes, 3-13-90). I recorded my perceptions of who I thought Maya, James, and Jil were in the classroom community and how this influenced my reading of Maya's text in my notes:

> The story can be read as a double-pronged attack on Jil and James, with different intents. The story is insulting to both Jil and James. Both read it that way themselves (or at least Maya anticipated James would and changed his first name). Unless you argue that they just wouldn't want to be in any text that Maya wrote, which is possible.
>
> The story is insulting to them on one level because of the boy/girl thing (teasing might be a better word). It's also insulting for Jil because she "wants zits," she embarrasses herself in front of the teacher, she doesn't have anyone to play with except for a boy (Jake/James), she gets beat up, and she gets kissed.

> For James, besides the insult of interacting with a girl, defending
> her, and kissing her, there is a status thing. Jil is not in the in group
> (does not play or work, as far as I know, with Lisa, Mary, Carol). There-
> fore, to be associated with Jil might be especially insulting.
>
> Maya's position seems closer to James than Jil—is this a sort of
> high-status teasing by suggesting a cool person likes an uncool per-
> son? Perhaps Maya is scoring points with friends for teasing a popular
> boy and slamming an unpopular girl. (Fieldnotes, 3-8-90)

I was assigning motives here and reading *for* children—highly spec-
ulative activities. Maya's text, with its references to zits and Jil and James,
had forced me to consider the rhetorical effects of a child's story. This
was the first time during the year that I had tried, in any sustained way,
to do such a reading. In an important sense, I began this book with the
attempt. From my work with these children across 6 or so months, I was
trying to determine possible meanings of the text in this particular setting. Possible meanings—I did not necessarily feel confident in my
assessments of social relations and local meanings at the time.

Would my response have been different if a different group of children were involved as author and characters? I am sure it would have
been. I might have attributed, for example, a defensive posture to Jessie
if she had authored the piece, instead of what seems the attribution—
correct or incorrect—of an offensive, aggressive posture on the part of
Maya. I worried a little about this attribution in my fieldnotes, both for
what it meant for my future relationship with Maya, and for what it said
about me and my past relations with Maya.

> So, ultimately, I'm thinking of censuring this piece because it feels ugly
> and hurtful. How do I say that to Maya? What effect does this have on
> her when I encourage her to write about things that she cares about,
> is interested in? And, to be truthful, I also have to ask about how my
> response is affected by my own relationship with Maya—I am often
> frustrated with her behavior in class, so am I using this text to get back
> at her a little, even if "justified?" (Fieldnotes, 3-8-90)

But it is unlikely that any author would have been allowed to share
The Zit Fit that day in class. Why? My response to Maya's text depended
upon one of the ways I had previously inserted myself into the social
relations of children in the writing workshop—a rule about names—and
that rule would have been in effect whoever the author was.

———

Almost from the beginning of the year, children wrote themselves, their
friends, and their enemies into stories. Students soon began voicing com-

plaints, and Grace and I also became concerned as we read some children's texts. Eventually, Grace told the children that they could not write anything mean about others. I agreed with Grace's intent—she wanted children to respect and not hurt one another—but not with the rule. I had two concerns. One was preserving the norm of student ownership. I wanted children to be able to write what they wanted, to control their own texts as far as was possible. And, at times, this might include writing mean things about others. This was connected to my second concern. Given my experience with children, I was worried about how they would interpret the word "mean." I wanted to leave a space open for anger and criticism in their writing—directed, perhaps, at authority figures, bullies.

The rule eventually put in place was more specific, and specific to our classroom. I invoked it with Maya immediately after the long pause in which I shifted my reading of her text. I said, "How do you think Jil is going to feel about her name being in it? *We should talk to Jil.*" I interpret some of Maya's responses—"Oh we told her" and "I've already changed James' name"—as at least partial acknowledgement of this rule, if not agreement with its use in this case. I gave a rough statement of the rule in my notes that night:

> I immediately invoked the rule that has emerged. To go public with a text, the names of characters must be approved by people in the room who have those names. (Fieldnotes, 3-8-90)

Quite a bit was at stake here. The rule attempted to balance protecting children's feelings and establishing a supportive classroom environment against student control of text. The rule assumed a private/public distinction: Children had control over writing they kept private (they could include other children's names in their stories). But if those stories were to go public, the use of children's names had to be approved by the children involved. Student control, versus teacher control, was served by this rule in another way. The rule did not depend on the teacher to determine the "meaning" of a particular writer's use of a child's name. That determination was left to the child. As a teacher, I tried to enforce the rule, lend my institutional authority to its enactment.

Another issue was involved here. The rule gave children control over the stories that were told about them, at least in public. Writing workshop approaches are based on the idea that children's own voices and stories should be heard in writing classrooms. But Graves, Calkins, and Murray do not seem to worry about children writing stories for others. The issue is: Who gets to tell whose story? The workshop provided a public sphere in which various individuals and groups defined themselves and others in their writing. Much like the struggles women, people of color, members of the working class, and others, have taken up to define themselves, to have their own tell their own stories (instead of white, elite males), there were struggles for definition of self within the workshop. Jil must have thought something was at stake when she wrote, "change the name from me to someone else."

With the rule about names, I tried to intervene in these struggles in order to give individual children control over the use of their own names in the workshop. Who threatened individual children's control of their names? Who threatened to silence certain children by making them the "objects" of someone else's stories, rather than the subjects of their own? My discussion, in chapter 5, of who did and did not write themselves explicitly into fictional texts as characters provides an answer—other children. And in particular, children with high status and power in the room. My examples there came from texts that were made public before I understood much about children's responses to seeing their names in other people's stories. The most striking example of children silencing other children, of reducing other children to "objects," was Mary and Suzanne's casting of John, Leon, and Robert as towers in their play. I shared Mary and Suzanne's text in the context of a discussion of public texts, so I probably misled you. That text did not go public.

And if I remained silent here, I could mislead you again, for good effect. But the rule about names did *not* impede their play's progress to larger audiences. When they first showed it to me, I did not pay much attention to their list of characters. Mary and Suzanne wanted to enter their play in a contest sponsored by a local theater group, and needed my signature on an application form that certified, among other things, that the play was the original work of the authors. With pen in hand, I learned that Suzanne and Mary copied their play out of a book in the school library. Actually, they condensed the adult author's play quite skillfully. Or, if you prefer, they appropriated her words for their own purposes. But that is another story.

But not entirely. The rule about names was supposed to give control over certain words—children's names—to the children who claimed them as their own. It was supposed to keep authors from appropriating other children's names for their own purposes, unless those children went along with the author's purposes. The rule had emerged, and I had enforced it, before I understood its significance. It "assumed" what I was just beginning to articulate for myself in my response to Maya's text—that children could turn their texts to purposes I had not anticipated, and that I could not support if I wanted all children to "come to voice" in the writing workshop.

There were problems with the rule. The public/private distinction was shaky, especially in a writing workshop in which children continually talked and shared their writing in collaborative projects and peer conferences. According to Maya, she and Carol had already told Jil about *The Zit Fit*, and possibly James as well. This could have been done during class, on the playground, or on the way home from school.

So the rule could not stop children from hurting each other. In fact, one thing I realized in this case was how, if Jil somehow had been isolated from Maya's story before, invoking the rule made her read the story. Jil's control over her name was bought at this price. And this was placed against her hearing the story read in front of the class, or seeing it published in the classroom library.

––––––

There were two primary ways for children to go public with their texts: sharing time and the writing workshop library. My response to Maya's text anticipated sharing time in at least two senses. First, I was talking to Maya just a few minutes before sharing time was to begin, and the conference was supposed to help Maya get ready for sharing. I had little time to read and figure out what should be done. Second, my response anticipated sharing time in the sense that I was worried about how children in the class—including Jil and James—would respond to Maya's text. Sharing time was a public, teacher-sponsored event. My response to Maya's text cannot be separated from my sense of responsibility for what happened there.

This deserves comment. Sharing time replaced the teacher at the front of the room with the child writer who read stories and solicited responses from peers. Grace and I encouraged and required children in the workshop to listen carefully to the texts shared by classmates. In this sense, we lent our institutional authority to the discourse of sharing time. In such situations, as Gilbert (1989) reminds us, children's stories become part of the official curriculum of the classroom, and thus, are deserving of our scrutiny for what they are "teaching." Maya wanted to share her text *publicly* in the writing workshop. That is what forced me to invoke the rule about names, and to worry about what Maya's text might mean to her classmates.

In an ideal writing conference, as in Habermas' (1970) ideal speech situation, we would expect an open-ended conversation between teacher and student in which various claims are raised and discussed, by both parties, in relation to the text at hand. The conference with Maya did not look much like this. I quickly decided that I could not allow Maya to read her text without Jil's response and time for me to look at her text more closely. Most of the conference has me telling Maya what will happen: I told her Jil would read the text, that I would read the text, and that Maya could share tomorrow. There was little exploration of what Maya wanted to do with this piece, what she thought of it, or what help she needed. I attribute this to the time constraints I felt, to my determination that a classroom rule applied in this situation, and to my own struggle to figure out what the responsible thing to do was. My power as a teacher and adult enabled me to dominate the conference as I did.

We were working under severe time constraints, when perhaps more time was needed in order to unravel and work through what was for me a puzzling and emotionally charged text. When I decided that the rule about names was important in this situation, that also constrained my and Maya's talk. One way it did this was by increasing the number of people who were involved in the situation, and whose perspectives would have to be taken into account. Instead of just Maya and me working something out between the two of us, I had decided that at least Jil and James needed to be in on the conversation, if not literally, then at least their interests considered. And in some sense, the function of the rule about names was to *stop* talk between the teacher and student, since the rule referred the question of whether or not a child's name appeared in a story to another child. That is, the rule called for a conversation among children, not necessarily one between teacher and student. In my conference with Maya, I looked away from Maya and our discussion, in order to bring Jil into our conversation.

Finally, I faced a great deal of uncertainty in relation to the meaning of Maya's text, and what I should do about it (beyond referring the question of names to children involved). I was faced with a text that drew on slippery, shifting things like social relations among children and local, timely meanings of words like "zits." Furthermore, if I was correct that at least part of Maya's intent was to hurt or tease other children, then it seems unlikely that our writing conference would be the place to expose and construct meaning in polite conversation. Maya would have good reason—given her knowledge of teacher disapproval of children hurting one another, and given her position of relatively little power in relation to me—to *conceal*, not reveal, possible meanings of her text; it would make sense for her to conceal her intention(s), rather than help me understand what her text and she were about.

That night, when I was no longer under the same time constraints or pressure to make a decision—when the situation was less "forced" (Scollon, 1988)—I could interact with and respond to Maya's text in ways that I had not earlier in the day.

I hadn't noticed at first that it is, formally, a fairly well-structured story. The boy/girl relationship sets up a series of problems that are eventu-

ally resolved with a man saving a woman and the woman getting a
kiss (sounds like I should be objecting to this on feminist grounds as
well). (Fieldnotes, 3-8-90)

I noticed how the story depended on the sorts of cultural knowledge
I had anticipated questioning in my conception of response as socioanalysis. At the beginning of the story, there was the suggestion that a
physical characteristic of Jil (acne), rather than, for example, her intelli-
gence or courage, was what would make her attractive to the man of her
choice. Later, against what her own experience told her, she believed
Jake when he said that the fat boys would not beat her up. Jil did get beat
up—this was a common occurrence, the author did not seem to take a
moral stance against it, and Jil was unwilling or unable to fight back
(something the third grade girls I worked with were usually quite able
and willing to do in fights with each other and with their third grade male
classmates). At the end, she was rescued (a little late, like in Charles
Bronson movies) by Jake, and was kissed by him. There was much in
Maya's text (more than I have noted) that is "traditionally given in gender and identity" (Willinsky, 1990), and that could have become the
focus of response and conversation.

But I did not pursue this line the next day in my second conference
with Maya. I was more concerned about the immediate consequences for
Jil and James of this story going public. I was also concerned about how
to talk with Maya about this, since I anticipated violating a norm of the
workshop that many children and I took quite seriously—student control
over their own texts.

Maya sat back in her chair, arms at her sides, hands pressing
against the seat of her chair. I tried to look at her, but sometimes had
trouble looking her in the face. I was fairly sure my reading of her
text was a good one, but I didn't like confronting Maya about it.
(Fieldnotes, 3-9-90)

I opened the conference with a sort of good news/bad news scenario.
The good news was that the story had a good structure—it set up problems for the characters and resolved them by the end. The bad news:

LENSMIRE: The problem I have with it is this, it's really mean. It's really
mean to the characters, it's really mean to Jil. And she, she, she said
that you can't use her name in it. I think people—
MAYA: What am I supposed to do, use an alien's name? It's not fair. I want
it to be somebody's name in the class. (Audiotape, 3-9-90)

I had said what I thought the meaning of Maya's text was for Jil and the class. Maya bristled. She returned to "I want it to be somebody's name in the class" repeatedly in our conference. At the time, I could not figure this out. One guess now is that she was using the word "somebody" to say she wanted to keep Jil as the character's name. In other words, it was a way of resisting my request that she take out Jil's name. Another guess is that James, and not Jil, was a primary target of Maya's text, and that she knew that in order for James to be properly teased by the story, there had to be a girl from the class in the other character's position. In other words, Maya knew what James himself knew when he wrote his first *Line Leader* with Ken: She knew that she could provoke response by suggesting a romantic relationship between boys and girls in the room. Perhaps Maya had learned this in part from James and Ken. In order to involve James in such a provocative situation, a girl from the class was needed.

In the conference, I answered her by saying that the story would be hurtful to whomever she placed in Jil's role. I listed the things that happened to the character—she liked zits, was embarrassed in class, beat up by boys—as reasons someone would not want to be that character. Finally, I asked her directly about her intentions, if she wanted to hurt someone's feelings with the story.

MAYA: It's just a story.
LENSMIRE: But what were you trying to do in this story? Why did you write *that* story?
MAYA: Because I liked it.

Maya answered and defended herself (and her text) against my questions with two short utterances that invoked powerful literary and workshop assumptions. Her first response, "It's just a story," points to the disjunction between author and material in fictional texts that I discussed in the last chapter. There, I emphasized how fiction lessened risks of personal exposure for authors, because readers of fiction could not assume that the author was expressing her own experiences or beliefs and values. But there is another consequence of the "distance" between authors and their material in fiction, one that Maya seemed to count on here. Britton (1982; again with quotes from Widdowson, 1975) provides part of Maya's defense:

> The literary writer, in fact . . . is "relieved from any social responsibility for what he says in the first person." (Love letters . . . count as evidence in a court of law, love poems don't!) (p. 158)

Maya did not write her story in first person, but with her first statement above, she asserted that her text was fictional, and by implication, that certain demands should not be made of it or her. It was *just a story*—she was not trying to tell about things that really happened to real people, so she should not be held accountable for lying or slandering. She was engaged in an acceptable sort of lying, and that lying included making up settings and characters and events. Maya had not written, to draw on Britton's example above, a letter to a friend, or to Jil herself, in which she said all sorts of nasty things about her. From this angle, my questions for Maya were inappropriate—I wanted to connect her story too closely to real children and real feelings, and hold her responsible for the effects of her story in the classroom.

At the heart of our conflict at that moment in our second writing conference, was the status of Maya's text in the world and her relationship to it. Maya and I represented two major opposing positions in literary theory on such questions, positions suggested by the traditional distinction between rhetoric and poetry:

> *Rhetoric* and *poetry*, the text that *means* and the text that *is*, the text for *persuasion* and the text for *contemplation*. . . . (Scholes, 1985, p. 77)

My position was one that emphasized the participation of Maya's text in the social life of the classroom. I asked Maya, "But what were you trying to do in this story?" I was emphasizing the rhetorical consequences of her text, and wanted to make sure she understood her text had effects on others. I aligned myself with literary theorists such as Bakhtin (1981), Said (1983), and others, who conceive of texts as "something we *do*, and indissociably interwoven with our practical forms of life" (Eagleton, 1983).

Maya's position, expressed in, "It's just a story," removed her text from the social life of the classroom, and removed her social responsibility for her text. Her position has a long tradition—in Romanticism (Williams, 1983), as well as support from more recent literary theories such as New Criticism and certain versions of deconstruction (such as de Man, 1979). Here, texts are creations of imagination, self-referential and solitary objects, sites for the play of indeterminate meaning, removed from the struggles and responsibilities of everyday life:

> At the center of the world is the contemplative individual self, bowed over its book, striving to gain touch with experience, truth, reality, history, or tradition. (Eagleton, 1983, p. 196)

Maya's second comment, in response to my question as to why she wrote that story, requires less attention, not because it is less important, but because it assumed a commitment of writing workshop approaches that I have already developed in some detail—individual student control of texts. Maya justified her text by saying, "Because I liked it." She asserted her right, in the writing workshop, to choose the texts she would write. In a setting in which children were encouraged to make their own individual choices, and the teachers worked to support student intention, Maya's text (usually) would need little more justification for being written and shared than that she liked it. The workshop's commitment to individual student intention, as Willinsky (1990) has shown, has roots in Romanticism. Thus, Maya's first and second comments express different aspects of a "poetic" conception of texts, in which the texts authors write are abstracted from the contexts of their production and consumption.

Maya and I had reached an impasse. Maya was set on having the character's name be someone in the class—this was her piece, she had the right to control it. And she wanted to share it. This was exactly what I felt I could not allow. I rejected the notion of Maya running from girl to girl in the class, looking for someone to take Jil's place (if nothing else, making the text public that way).

LENSMIRE: Well, I'm not going to let you share that story as it is right now, because I'm afraid it would hurt people's feelings. But if you want to try to make changes to it that you think would make it better, that way, you can, okay? Or, you can find, I know you have a lot of other stories, because you write a lot. So what are you going to do? What do you want to do?

MAYA: I have to change the name. I suppose I have to change the name.

Maya said this slowly and grudgingly. She gave in to me—I do not believe she had been persuaded—and agreed to not name the character after Jil or other children in the class. I talked to her about the first part, about the zits. Maya told me that Carol had named it *The Zit Fit,* so I told her that she could just name it something else then and change the first part. I ignored the other aspects of the text I found questionable; I even said that the rest of the story was fine, which was not necessarily true. I wish I could say that I had made a well-reasoned decision that we had dealt with enough for now, but I just forgot. Maya did not look too pleased as she left the table; I did not feel too happy myself.

The story is not over, but not because Maya continued to pursue this text. The next time I conferenced with her, she was working on a text describing a game she and her brother played together. It was Carol's turn.

Alongside each utterance . . . off-stage voices can be heard. (Barthes, 1974)

After Maya and I finished our conference, I worked at the round table. I looked up when I heard Carol, two rows over from me with Maya just behind her, almost shouting at me, "That's unfair!" She said this several times before I understood what she was talking about. Then she said, "It's just a name." I ignored her and looked back at my work.

The next Monday, I overheard Carol and Maya attempting to enlist their regular teacher, Grace, on their side. Carol told Grace that Maya should be allowed to use Jil's name in the story. Grace left them and walked over to me. Before Grace got to me, Carol called out after her, "Jil is a popular name." Grace told me that she had told them they had to respect their classmates. I told Grace that I wanted the same thing. While we were talking, Carol said, "Okay, then we'll just put it backwards—LIJ." Carol and Maya continued talking, just loud enough for Grace and me to hear, and probably Jil as well, who sat a few feet behind them. They seemed to be accomplishing orally what I was not allowing them to do with Maya's written text.

> Tuesday:
> The Carol and Maya "It's just a name" saga continues. Today the attack shifted. Somewhere in here, Carol and Maya noticed that Jil had written on Maya's text—"change the name from me." Now Carol said, "How dare Jil write on Maya's paper" (she actually said, "How dare.") She was about three or four feet away from me, arms at her side, fists clenched, with a lot of indignation on her face, body slightly bent forward from the waist. I didn't get it right away, but I soon realized what she was talking about.
> Today I took her on. I told her that I wasn't going to back down. That it was a classroom rule that people could take their names out of other people's stories before the stories went public. Carol responded that it still was not right for Jil to write on Maya's paper. I told her that I had asked Jil to respond, she had, and that it wouldn't happen that way again. She said it still wasn't right. As she walked away, she said that Jil wasn't the nice person we teachers thought she was, "not such a nice person at all." But she seemed somewhat subdued. Maybe from my tone of voice she realized that I was serious. (Fieldnotes, 3-9-90)

Whatever purposes Carol had for arguing with me, she assumed that a student's text was her private possession. She assumed student ownership. And she used this norm as a resource to argue with me—how dare Jil write on Maya's paper. Graves (1981) had introduced his concept of student ownership with a little story about how renters and owners acted differently toward the houses in which they lived—owners took better care of them. He believed student ownership of texts resulted in better quality products because, like homeowners, students who owned their texts would care for them more, in the crafting of their material and their attention to surface features. Apparently, Carol and Maya looked upon Jil's comment, written in the margin of Maya's paper, as an unsightly bit of graffiti.

In any event, this was the last time Carol confronted me about this issue. Conferences with Carol about her work seemed, to me at least, largely unaffected by all this. Carol continued writing long texts and talking with me regularly.

I talked with Maya's mother, Lauren, at parent-teacher conferences at the end of March. I knew Lauren better than most of the other parents— for the first few months of school, Lauren had helped children put together and publish their books in the workshop. We had had the chance to talk about what I was trying to do in my teaching, and Lauren responded positively to what I said and what she saw happening in the classroom. During our conference, I told Lauren that Maya and I had had a run-in over a text I thought would be hurtful to others. Lauren's response was supportive. She told me that she had been concerned, after talking with me about writing workshop approaches, that children would be granted control over their writing without taking on any responsibility for what they wrote. Her only question for me was, did Maya understand why I had questioned her piece? I told Lauren that I had talked with Maya about how I thought her story would hurt other children's feelings.

But Lauren's question cannot be answered quite as simply as I answered it that night. If by "understand" we mean something approaching Habermas' (1984, 1987) notion of reaching agreement, I doubt that Maya understood. I depended, ultimately, on my institutional authority to settle what would happen. I had begun questioning student intention and material with Maya, and she and Carol questioned my intervention in Maya's writing. But the process was most likely terminated long before Maya and I had talked enough to explain ourselves to each other.

I do not want to imply, however, that all difficulty in this case arose from complexity and misunderstanding—that if only we had had the time and the knowledge, everything would have run along smoothly. This story was also about a conflict of wills and beliefs and values. I think that, in some ways, Maya and Carol and I understood each other quite well, that Maya understood my concerns about her story, but rejected the normative claim I was making that it was not all right to share that sort of story. And if her intentions were not entirely honorable, then she had reasons for hiding those intentions and not engaging me in an open discussion of her text.

I acted to keep a text that I decided would be hurtful to other children from going public. My response was caught up in questions of how we should treat one another, who gets to tell whose stories, and social relations among children. I decided that following the child would be morally and politically irresponsible.

But response as socioanalysis suffered here as well, for at least two reasons. First, the commitment to looking to the past, to addressing the distorted stories children bring with them from outside the classroom, ignores the life, the culture in which children participate in schools. Maya's text included material worth examining for what it said about women and their relations to men in our society. But in this case, the immediate relations among children were more pressing. Second, the powerful image of response as an intimate, isolated conversation, involving two people and a text, ignores all the ways teacher response itself participates in the social life of the classroom. In this instance, my response to Maya's text included conversations with Jil, Carol, Maya's mother, and Grace; it responded to a text written by Suzanne and the teasing Jessie encountered; it drew on readings of who children were to each other, and classroom norms; and it anticipated the responses of future readers of Maya's texts, as well as Maya's responses to what I said.

I have tried to suggest throughout my discussion the tentativeness of my interpretation of this case and the meanings of what people said and did. If things were tentative here, they were even more so while I was teaching, and that was an important problem in this occasion for response. My decision to not follow Maya's lead represented a fairly hard stand on soft ground. Following the child would have been easier; treating the text as a cultural artifact of American society would have been easier. Reading and responding to Maya's text in relation to this particular context was much harder.

Chapter 7

Workshop Re-Visions

[Writing workshop teachers] want the child to control, take charge
of information in his writing. Their craft is to help the child to main-
tain control for himself. That is the craft of teaching. They stand as
far back as they can observing the child's way of working, seeking
the best way to help the child realize his intentions.

Donald H. Graves
Writing: Teachers and Children at Work

Perhaps we need to turn to the unsung sisters of these cherubic
boys for redemption. But in order to discover how our daughters
redeem us, we must forsake the innocent child, free of knowledge
and guile, for the one who lies. "A child should always say what's
true / And speak when he is spoken to," chides Robert Louis
Stevenson. Both the act and its admonishment testify to the con-
trivance that is the innocence of childhood.

Madeleine R. Grumet
Bitter Milk: Women and Teaching

James, Maya, and their friends, were worldly children pursuing social
projects. They were sophisticated and strategic, with complex and sometimes questionable intentions. From their elevated position within the
peer culture, they often looked to the immediate classroom for material—they laughed with and at their peers and teachers, affirmed friendships and divisions among children with their talk and texts, and accom-
modated and resisted teacher interventions into their projects. They were
the "wily, winsome, wise, wild, and whining creatures who are our kids"
(Grumet, 1988, p. 156). They were also more or less hostile audiences for
other children, and their projects, in and out of the classroom, were
partly what made them so.

Writing workshop advocates need to forget James and Maya, as well as Jessie and John, in order to write their how-to books. They remember and narrate innocent children pursuing private projects. Innocent, not so much in what they know (for these writers know that children have experience in the world), but in their actions and relations with others—simple, straightforward, transparent, and with the best of intentions. These children pursue private projects, directed at objects outside the classroom, to personal pasts and interests—family and pet happenings, the space shuttle, record collections. In my early dreams of "heteroglossic" writing workshops sounding with the unofficial voices of children—dreams that drew heavily on the Romantic images of solitary child writers provided by Calkins (1983) and Graves (1986) and others—the voices of children are like oblique lines in geometry, connecting children to objects with straight lines that never intersect and that exist on alternative planes.

Such a vision is a rather strange appropriation of Bakhtin's (1981) concept of heteroglossia. "Heteroglossic" does point to the presence of multiple, divergent voices, but *with* these voices in constant contact and interaction, involved in a struggle for meaning that began when we mouthed our (parents') first words. Bakhtin's "line" from author to object (to audience)—the word—is tangled with others' words, stretched at times to breaking:

> The word, directed toward its object, enters a dialogically agitated and tension-filled environment of alien words, value judgements, and accents, weaves in and out of complex interrelationships, merges with some, recoils from others, intersects with yet a third group: and all this may crucially shape discourse, may leave a trace in all its semantic layers. (p. 276)

The dialogically agitated environment of our writing workshop was a site of struggle over identity, participation, meaning, and values. In their talk and texts, children took up conflicting positions on questions of who should tell whose stories, who should speak and be listened to, whose interpretations are valid, how it is we should treat one another.

Traditional writing instruction, paralleling usual classroom discourse (Cazden, 1986), locks the student into a teacher-controlled pattern in which the teacher assigns writing, the student writes in response, and the teacher evaluates. Workshop approaches attempt to disrupt this pattern in at least two ways. Through student selection of topics, the child makes the first move in an interaction that places the teacher, ideally, in the position of response. But workshop approaches also break a teacher-dominated discourse by allowing and encouraging children to turn away from the teacher, front and center, to each other. In place of a traditionally unauthentic, fault-finding teacher-audience, workshops promote an authentic, meaning-finding one, and peers are a significant part of that audience.

Workshop approaches flood classroom discourse with the voices of children, as children write, talk to the teacher and to each other, and read and respond to each other's texts. But workshop advocates have attempted to capture these very real, vigorous children on the page with a Romantic rhetoric that tends to abstract authors and texts from their social contexts. Children write from their personal experience, and the choices of how and why to write, and on what topics, are assumed to be made on the basis of personal interest and meaningfulness. Children need an authentic audience so the writing is real, but workshop advocates seldom consider the ways audience can shape and constrain the writing of even young children (Berlin, 1988; Elbow, 1987).

For workshop advocates, the writer's struggle is the effective expression of something that is inside. They have "happily taken the personal and public aspects of literacy to consist of a one-way street: the individual finds a vehicle in writing for those deep and hidden thoughts at the core of the self and goes increasingly public with them" (Willinsky, 1990, p. 208). Lost in such a conception of written literacy is the sensitivity of authors to the social contexts within which they work. We forget that all of this writing is going on in schools, in which students are expected to work and teachers are expected to make sure they do; forget that peers are deliberately significant audiences for the writing done by children in writing workshops.

Atwell (1987), a workshop advocate who writes from her teaching experiences with eighth graders, acknowledges the importance of peers for her students' writing:

> In considering the realities of adolescence, if we know that social relationships come first, it simply makes good sense to bring those relationships into the classroom and put them to work. . . . Within the structure of a writing workshop, students decide who can give the kind of help they need as they need it . . . small groups form and disband in the minutes it takes for a writer to call on one or more other writers, move to a conference corner, share a piece or discuss a problem, and go back to work with a new perspective on the writing. (p. 41)

Atwell's portrayal of peer relations in writing workshops is like those of other workshop advocates—it casts peer relations only in a positive light, and suggests an openness and fluidity of association among students that my own experiences and research with children tend to contradict. My worry is that this fluidity is only apparent, that beneath it are more stable patterns of peer relations among children that divide them, subordinate some to others, routinely deny certain children the help and support that others receive from peers.

When I loosened the lid on student intentions and association in my classroom, peers became extremely important influences on student experiences and writing. These influences were not all positive. Peers were sources of support and confidence. They were also sources of conflict and risk, and pushed back on the writing children did in the classroom. Children evaluated and excluded each other—by gender, by social class, by personality—in ways that echoed some of the worst sorts of divisions and denigrations in our society. Children divided themselves up, sometimes in less disturbing, more temporary ways, in ways that allowed for changing evaluations, new friends and enemies. But they did, at any given moment and with more or less permanency, differentiate among their peers in terms of who was and who was not a friend, a desirable collaborator, a trusted audience in conferences and sharing time.

Peers, as audiences for children's writing, brought with them friendship, trust, a "social energy" (Dyson, 1989) that could empower young writers and their writing in the classroom. Peers also brought with them teasing, risk, and conflict. Both aspects of peers-as-audience were important for student experiences. I have tended to emphasize the latter, since so little is said about this aspect of children's experiences in writing workshops.

But if James and Maya taught us anything, it is that writers in the workshop were not just pushed around by their audiences—they pushed back. As writers, children were not *only* vulnerable (susceptible to influence, confronted with risks), they were also assertive. They took evaluative positions, expressed interests, valued this and not that. Their texts were not just more or less well-executed expressions of personal experience and objects of contemplation; they were rhetorical, had effects, did work. Children's texts could influence others' conceptions of themselves and their worlds, could make them laugh, hurt them, make them feel connected to others, safe or unsafe, encourage them to speak and write, or remain silent.

The rhetoric of workshop approaches does not entirely ignore the rhetorical nature of children's texts. Calkins (1986) asserts that a "sense of authorship comes from the struggle to put something big and vital in print, and from seeing one's own printed words reach the hearts and minds of readers" (p. 9). But it seems that, for Calkins and the others, the words from children that reach others' hearts and minds will never be false or hurtful or ugly. Their teaching depends on it, since workshop teachers follow children, support their intentions.

Gilbert (1989) aligns writing workshop approaches with child-centered commitments, and Romantic conceptions of creativity and imagination. She argues that the

> Seemingly innocent discourse about student authorship, student literature and student ownership of texts needs much closer scrutiny. By constructing an elaborate edifice of personal artistic creativity over school writing, the discourse masks the ideological nature of the production of school texts. The act of creation, the individual expression of personal experience, becomes the focus of attention. . . . The messages these texts carry are incidental. (p. 199)

I learned about the rhetorical nature of children's texts because the messages they carried for children in my room were anything but incidental. These messages were continuous with the talk and other actions of children in the classroom—interactions that silenced Jessie, enraged John, amused James.

I opened this chapter with quotes arranged to play Grumet against Graves. Grumet (1988) has a less Romantic view of children, and she would take the messages of children's stories seriously. But her response to the problem of schools "requiring order and stillness, replacing touch with the exchange of performance for grades" (p. 162)—her response to an educational system aimed at producing "child redeemers," the innocent sons who would liberate us adults from our adult world—is similar in tone to that of writing workshop advocates. Grumet looks to the possibilities of daughters' lies, their fantasies of how things could be, for their redemptive power, and couches at least parts of her proposal in the most Romantic of imagery—gardens and growing plants.

> In showing us the world as they would have it, they reveal the world that we fled because we were not brave enough to pitch our tents and raise our flags there. Their lies can become our knowledge . . . the child's fantasies can flower in the fictive ground of the curriculum. . . . School is not the real world, and so it shares the property that Marianne Moore attributes to poetry: "imaginary gardens with real toads in them." (p. 162)

Grumet is responsible enough to remember that if we want children to transform our world, "we had better transform theirs." She is honest enough to remember that all lies are not "pleasant and pastoral," but says little about what to do with such lies when they grow in the garden of lies you are tending. And what about lies with vines and leaves that choke other lies and keep them from the sun?

It is time to look to the future, to our futures in classrooms, and ask what the experiences of children in my room mean for how we teach and learn writing. If my classroom was a philosophical laboratory in which I brought theory to bear on practice, it is time for practice to bear down a little on theory. In the remainder of this chapter, I suggest two re-visions for the work of teachers and children in writing workshops. The first is a new conception of teacher response to children's writing, one that recognizes the connectedness of response to the social life of children in the classroom, and that actively strives to create a classroom community in which children accept and learn from each other's differences. With this re-vision, I continue the work, begun in chapter 1, of articulating a critical stance, a position, from which we might respond responsibly to the lives and texts of children. The second re-vision is to strengthen the role of the teacher as curriculum-maker in the writing workshop, by having teachers engage children in collective writing projects focused on important texts in children's lives.

I do not provide full-blown discussions and evaluations of these proposals. Future work will have to explore, for example, the multiple, concrete ways that we can establish and sustain the sort of classroom community I advocate below, and examine the special risks and opportunities that collective writing projects pose for the voice and agency of individual children. My purpose is to offer these re-visions as possible directions for the future development of workshop approaches.

Workshop advocates conceive of response as something a teacher does in relation to a particular child and his oral and written texts, as an action taken in isolation from the immediate context within which teachers and students work. The goal of response is to help the child be better able to realize his intentions in text, both immediately and in the future. I had a slightly more complicated vision of response when I started my teaching. I realized that there would be times when it would be irresponsible to support student intentions, in as much as children would sometimes draw on material—such as racist or sexist stereotypes—that needed to be questioned.

I had appropriated and developed rules for response. Rule one: Follow the child, support her intentions. Rule two: When the material was questionable, question it without taking away control of the writing from the child. I brought these rules for response to my work with children, and found they provided me precious little guidance in the blur of children, texts, and classroom situations. I learned the inadequacy of following the child and socioanalysis, as conceptions of response, for capturing what was involved when teachers and children talked about texts in writing conferences.

Children's intentions for writing are neither necessarily transparent, nor supportable. If we locate children in a mix of social relations and texts that influence their work, then to conceive of an individual child as somehow having a simple, clear-cut intention that we can identify and follow is a problem. Writers pursue many intentions in their works that are more or less conscious to them—a student writer may, simultaneously, hope to tease her friends, want to become a better writer, and try to please her teacher (Hulbert, 1987). Writers are influenced by, and in some sense, their intentions are shared with, their audience. Romantic conceptions of writers and writing simplify intention by assuming an isolated, preexistent self with preexisting intentions, rather than a social, emerging self, appropriating this, objecting to that, constructing itself and its intentions as it goes along: "Writing is not simply a tool we use to express a self we already have; it is a means by which we form a self to express" (Harris, 1987, p. 161). Consequently, as teachers, we continually shape children's intentions, not just follow them. And our influence can point intentions in different directions, toward varying ends.

Furthermore, children's intentions, even emerging ones, may not be transparent because children want to keep them hidden from us. Workshop advocates assume that children always want us to follow them, to understand what they are up to. Or put another way, they assume that children will never pursue intentions in writing that children would not want to explain to us, and that we could not support when they finished explaining.

I assumed that there would be occasions in which I could not support student intentions, and such considerations led to my conception of response as socioanalysis. But the critical stance I created there abstracted children's texts from the immediate classroom community, and proposed reading them as artifacts of a classist, racist, sexist society. This sort of response is important if we want to help our children avoid modes of thought and action that perpetuate these aspects of our society. But socioanalysis is inadequate, because it does not concern itself with local meanings, values, and relations, the micropolitics of particular classrooms and children's texts.

In my experiences as a teacher with these young children, I learned lessons that parallel what feminist theorists such as Gilligan (1982) and Benhabib (1992) have been trying to teach more traditional moral theorists—that issues of justice do not exhaust the moral domain, and should be complemented by attention to the relations and responsibilities of nurturing and caring for others. Gilligan writes that

Since everyone is vulnerable both to oppression and to abandon-
ment, two moral visions—one of justice, and one of care—recur in
human experience. The moral injunctions, not to act unfairly toward
others, and not to turn away from someone in need, capture these
different concerns. (cited in Benhabib, 1992, p. 189)

In my thinking about socioanalysis, I understood that teacher
response to children's texts was caught up in questions of justice—with
fairness, equality—inasmuch as I was concerned with helping children
avoid stereotypical representations of people by race, class, and gender
in their texts. What I didn't understand was that teacher response was
also bound up in the intimate relations of particular children with each
other, peer relations that nurtured some, and abandoned others. Our
workshop community was not an equally caring one for all children—
teacher response could intervene in or acquiesce to that community.

A more adequate conception of response, then, would address two
aspects of writing workshops that have been largely ignored. First, it
would pay more attention to the immediate peer culture, to social relations among children and the meanings and values they assign to each
other, texts, and teachers. The peer culture is an important backdrop
upon which children's texts are written and given their local, particular
meanings. Workshop approaches encourage teachers to know children,
but this is usually thought of as knowing individual children, as if these
individuals were not caught up in relations with each other (see, for
example, Graves, 1983, on individual children's "unique territories of
information," pp. 22–28). I am not denying the need for knowledge of
individual children. I am arguing that such a focus can blind us to the
ways children are connected to each other, blind us to the more or less
shared meanings and values children bring to their activities and texts.

Second, an adequate conception of response would include goals
that go beyond supporting (and/or questioning) student intentions. It
would include a vision of the type of classroom community in which we
want our children to write and learn. Workshop approaches have aligned
their goals with individual children's intentions, without considering that
the ends some children pursue may not be beneficial for other children
(or even themselves). There are bullies on the playground, and peer cul-
tures maintaining divisions among children by class, race, and gender.
We affirm these aspects of children's lives when we commit ourselves to
uncritically supporting student intentions. As Goodman (1992) has noted,

Given our cultural values, putting an emphasis on increasing the
personal freedom of students will probably result in anti-social, ego-

tistical posturing among children rather than the free child so often lauded in the radical school literature. Children's true individuality (rather than their self-indulgence) can grow only within a community structure in which there are restrictions and expectations placed upon the individual by that community. (p. 102)

My students and I created a community within the writing workshop, and children's writing emerged from and contributed to that community. The community we created was important for the experiences and learning of the children and teachers there. I have discussed some of its disturbing aspects. If, as Harris (1989) asserts, we "write not as isolated individuals but as members of communities whose beliefs, concerns, and practices both instigate and constrain, at least in part, the sorts of things we can say" (p. 12), then we had better pay attention to the classroom communities we create.

My first proposed re-vision for our teaching in writing workshops, then, is that teacher response to children's texts be *critically pragmatic*, and aimed at promoting an *engaged, pluralistic classroom community*. Critically pragmatic response is concerned with the intellectual, moral/political, and aesthetic fruits of children's texts, both for authors and audiences (Cherryholmes, 1988, 1990). An engaged, pluralistic classroom community is one that recognizes and affirms differences among children, and encourages children to learn from, be enhanced by, those differences.

This new conception of response has strong affinities to my previous ones, especially response as socioanalysis. Critically pragmatic response emphasizes engaging children in serious conversations about the meanings of their texts. It calls for the examination, with children, of what their texts have to say about who they are, what the world is like, and their relations to it and to each other. Unlike socioanalysis, which looked only to an oppressive society for questionable material, a critical pragmatic response would also pay attention to local, classroom relations and meanings. Furthermore, since texts go public in the writing workshop, the rhetorical play of a child's texts in the classroom community would be an important consideration and topic of discussion in writing conferences.

Maya's story, *The Zit Fit*, forced me to consider the rhetorical effects of her text on other children. I had to decide whether or not I would, above all, support individual student intention. I decided that there were other things to consider, such as how Maya's text would make Jil feel, and the messages I would be sending children about how we should treat each other in the workshop. The worth of Maya's project, then, was not judged solely on its importance or meaningfulness to Maya. It was also judged for how it participated in the classroom community.

Critically pragmatic response to children's texts would be guided by a sense of what sort of community we wanted to encourage and support in the classroom. I have adapted the notion of an engaged, pluralistic class- room community from Bernstein (1988). In his text, Bernstein character- ized what he called the "ethos" of pragmatism in the writings of Pierce, James, Dewey, and others. For Bernstein, an important theme of the prag- matist ethos was the vision of a community of inquirers that supported critical thought and action by its members. He addressed his text to the community of American philosophers (it was a presidential address to the American Philosophical Association), and argued that their community would do well to attempt to live out this pragmatist vision of community.

The central characteristics of an engaged, pluralistic classroom com- munity are suggested by its name. "Pluralistic" recognizes the diversity of children in classrooms, along lines of class, race, and gender, as well as attributes unique to specific individuals. It recognizes the heteroglossia of the voices of children in the classroom, the multiple social and personal intonations and evaluations that children bring to speaking and writing. But the fact that a community is pluralistic is less important than how it responds to that pluralism, what it does with it:

> For there is a danger of a *fragmenting* pluralism where centrifugal forces become so strong that we are only able to communicate with the small group that already shares our own biases, and no longer even experience the need to talk with others outside this cir- cle. . . . There is a *polemical* pluralism where the appeal to plural- ism doesn't signify a genuine willingness to listen and learn from others, but becomes rather an ideological weapon to advance one's own orientation. There is *defensive* pluralism, a form of tokenism, where we pay lip service to others "doing their own thing" but are already convinced that there is nothing important to be learned from them. (Bernstein, 1988, p. 15)

An engaged pluralistic classroom community embraces a different, more desirable, response to pluralism than the responses listed above. I use the word "engaged" to suggest three characteristics of the work and lives of children and teachers in such a community.

First, engaged refers to the participation of *all* children in the com- munity's important activities. It carries, then, the political connotations of voice that I discussed in chapter 1. Being engaged, like coming to voice, refers to children asserting themselves in public spaces, having their stories told and listened to by the class. If children are to learn from and about each other, to learn through their differences as well as their similarities, this participation is essential.

> It is the other who makes us aware both of her concreteness and her otherness. Without engagement, confrontation, dialogue and even a "struggle for recognition" in the Hegelian sense, we tend to constitute the otherness of the other by projection and fantasy or ignore it in indifference. (Benhabib, 1992, p. 168)

Teacher response, here, would look for ways to help and encourage children (such as Jessie and Karen) to make their texts available to larger audiences, and have those texts taken seriously.

Second, engaged refers to children paying attention to the needs of others in their immediate classroom community, learning to care for each other (Gilligan, 1982). When I talked with Maya about her story, I was asking her to consider the consequences of her text for other children. I was asking her to listen to and be concerned for another, particular child—Jil—who Maya apparently did not feel she had to consider.

Finally, engaged refers to the teacher's participation in this community, and recognizes the teacher's responsibility for encouraging and sustaining this, and not that, classroom community. It recognizes that the teacher will use her power as an adult and teacher in the classroom to influence the beliefs, concerns, and practices of the members of that community. At times, as in the Maya case, the teacher will restrict student action that could harm other children, and undermine the goal that all children actively participate in the making and remaking of the classroom community through the stories they tell and the responses they give to each other.

But teacher engagement, like student engagement, also refers to the teacher being open to, learning from, and caring for the children he works with. When the teacher is engaged with children, he is enriched by the fictional worlds they create on the page, and gains insights into his own and others' lives as he listens to children talk and interpret their own. He has the responsibilty to care for children, nurture their growth, enrich their lives.

Critically pragmatic response to children's texts would concern itself with the consequences of children's texts, both for the children who write them, and those who read them. Such response would seek to support a classroom community

> based upon mutual respect, where we are willing to risk our own prejudgments, are open to listening and learning from others, and we respond to others with responsiveness and responsibility. (Bernstein, 1988, p. 18)

I have proposed critically pragmatic response to children's texts as one re-vision to writing workshop approaches. My second re-vision is greater teacher participation in the determination of the writing projects children pursue in the classroom. Specifically, I suggest that teachers frame collective writing projects focused on important texts in children's lives. Our goals to support student voice and to create engaged, pluralistic classroom communities with children may be well served by such projects.

In my sketch of this re-vision, I first discuss Scholes' (1985) notion of textual power, as a reminder of why we should care about children coming to voice in writing workshops, and concern ourselves with the ends to which children put their voices. Then, I criticize the curriculum-work writing workshop approaches have envisioned for teachers and students in the past, and discuss an alternative.

———————

Scholes (1985) writes of textual power as "the power to select (and therefore to suppress), the power to shape and present certain aspects of human experience" (p. 20). In the selection of this and not that, in the particular slant and tone a writer takes, certain things are being valued over others, saying this is (and this is not) important, the truth, beautiful. Scholes argues that textual power should be the focus of our work with students and texts:

> We have always known this, but in the past we have often been content to see this power vested in the single literary work, the verbal icon, and we have been all too ready to fall down and worship such golden calves so long as we could serve as their priests and priestesses. We must help our students come into their own powers of textualization. We must help them see that every poem, play, and story is a text related to others, both verbal pretexts and social subtexts, and all manner of posttexts including their own responses, whether in speech, writing, or action. The response to a text is itself always a text. Our knowledge is itself only a dim text that brightens as we express it. (p. 20)

I like Scholes' conception of textual power for its location of meaning in the *interaction* of texts and people. He avoids, as I often did not in my early thinking about voice, the Romantic move to locate meaning primarily in the self-expression of an isolated author. The author is always writing in response to the words she was born into and within which she learned to think and speak. In response, she selects and appropriates others' words and gives them, with more or less effectiveness and courage, her own characteristic slant or "intonation" (Bakhtin, 1981).

It is also important that Scholes uses the word "power." Texts have the power to shape our conceptions of the world and our relations to each other. Their power is tied up with seeing the world in some ways and not others. Writing workshop advocates have largely avoided considering the good and bad such power can work. One way they have done this, as I have suggested in earlier chapters, is by construing the child as capable of only innocent intentions and content. They would have teachers efface themselves before children's texts, rather than truly engage them by considering their content. A second way they have avoided questions of power is to focus on the authors of texts, and not their audiences; to treat texts primarily as expressions of personal creativity, rather than rhetorical objects. One gets the sense that children's texts in workshops are important, but primarily to the people who write them, not to those who read them. It is important that other children read these texts, but not because they might enjoy them or learn something. Rather, the author needs an audience. Workshop approaches ignore the work texts do in the world:

> We care about texts for many reasons, not the least of which is that they bring us news that alters our way of interpreting things. If this were not the case, the Gospels and the teachings of Karl Marx would have fallen upon deaf ears. Textual power is ultimately power to change the world. (Scholes, 1985, p. 165)

My stories of James, Maya, and others, were stories about textual power put to various ends. One moral of those stories is that teachers must participate in shaping the ends toward which textual power is put by children. A laissez-faire attitude may very well allow status and power differences from the playground and society to assert themselves in the official work of the writing workshop. Children who are still learning about the consequences of their actions may hurt themselves and others in the process. Teacher response to children's texts is one way to influence the ends of children's textual power. Another is through collective writing projects.

Workshop approaches have traditionally focused on individual children pursuing individual projects. More recently, Calkins (1991) and her colleagues have begun to experiment with what they call "genre studies." In genre studies, the teacher and children in workshops focus, at various points during the year, on reading and writing a particular genre (for example, biography). Genre studies are examples of what I am calling collective writing projects. By this, I simply mean projects that a teacher and students pursue more or less together, as a class. They could focus on producing some type of group product, such as a student magazine, or focus on individual products connected by a common theme or problem. Genre studies place a particular genre of texts at the center of the work of teachers and students in the writing workshop.

I think the idea of genre studies is an important development. It recognizes that children may benefit from being able to produce some kinds of texts that they would not choose or even have access to without teacher intervention (Florio-Ruane & Lensmire, 1989; Martin, 1989). Writing workshop approaches have traditionally assumed that teacher determination of topics and genres for student writing necessarily undermines children's motivations to write and their development as writers. Hogan (1987), a teacher-researcher strongly influenced by workshop approaches, argues against such a view. In her work with college freshmen, she found that some students tended to fall back on what they could do or knew well, seldom challenging themselves with new topics or forms. My work, which highlights the importance of risk and peer influence in children's writing processes and texts, cautions us from assuming that children are unconstrained in their writerly decisions once teacher restrictions on topic or form are removed. Thus, teacher-assigned genres and topics may not be limiting, but actually expand student chances for growth in writing.

Genre studies are a new, positive development for workshop approaches. But from the standpoint of the purposes reading and writing might serve in writing workshops, they are not new at all. For workshop advocates are again avoiding critical work with the content, the messages of texts. Students have been the determiners of content in the workshop. Teachers have been responsible for a craft curriculum, for sharing tricks of the trade with young writers. The move to genre studies simply continues this emphasis: Part of the curriculum for which teachers are responsible is teaching children about formal aspects of texts and their production. This is important, and is surely part of helping children acquire textual power, helping them understand how texts are put together, how they work. But what is missing is any real concern with the ideas, values, and interests that texts express. Literature, and its reading, interpretation, and criticism, must become a more important part of workshop approaches.

It is not that literature has not been a significant part of the curriculum of writing workshops. Graves and Calkins want children to be surrounded by literature written by children and adults. But for what purpose(s)? An extended quote from Graves (1983) should help here:

> At every turn the teacher seeks to have children live the literature.
> The most important living occurs at the point at which children
> make literature themselves through writing. . . . Teachers try to
> make the literature "live" by bringing in authors, showing drafts and
> the processes by which authors write. They share their own writing
> and the drafts used to arrive at final products. They read about how
> authors compose, finding drafts of their work, or statements by chil-
> dren's authors about how they compose their books for chil-
> dren. . . . The mystique of authorship is removed that children
> may find out the beauty and depth of information contained in lit-
> erature itself. It is removed that children might learn to think and
> experience the joys of authorship themselves. (pp. 75, 76)

This quote from Graves captures some of the most progressive
aspects of writing workshop approaches. The idea that teachers should
"demystify" authorship is crucial for our attempts to help children take on
the role of author, and assert their power to shape and order the world
in that role. Graves and workshop advocates want to share the "beauty
and depth of information" of literature, its cognitive and aesthetic power,
with children; a vision that stands in stark contrast to the piles of work-
sheets many children face each day in reading and language arts classes.

But I am frustrated with Graves' discussion of literature here, for similar reasons that I was frustrated with Murray's (1985) discussion of writing conferences. Writing conferences, if you remember, were supposed
to be "professional discussions" among writers about "what works" in the
texts students produce. Where is criticism? Workshop advocates embrace
only the most limited senses of the term—a piece's effectiveness in relation to its intentions, or its success or failure in relation to "literary norms
of its mode or genre" (Scholes, 1985, p. 23). Writing is a craft, granted.
But writing is also an ideological activity, in that it involves meaning,
world views, moral and political positions that select and bend facts
toward particular ends (Volosinov, 1973; Eagleton, 1991).

Lost then, in workshop approaches' uses of literature, is any real
concern with ideas, values, and their relation to what sort of world we
hope to live in and how we want to treat and be treated by others. Lost
is any serious attention to criticism, as a "critique of the themes developed in a given fictional text, or a critique of the codes themselves, out
of which a given text has been constructed" (Scholes, 1985, p. 23). Criticism involves evaluating a text's themes and codes against a system of
values. It involves "human, ethical, and political reactions" to the meanings of texts.

Another type of collective writing project, then, is needed. In addition to those projects, such as genre studies, that focus on helping chil-

dren produce certain forms or genres of texts, children should also have opportunities to read and write, critically, *in response* to texts (of course, certain genres—such as reviews—are largely defined by such a critical response). In other words, children would read biographies not only in order to write them, or to learn skills of the craft of writing (as important as this work is); they would also read biographies in order to write responses to the subject's treatment of children, or critiques of the biographer's treatment of the subject. Grumet (1988) points to the purpose of making such work an important part of the writing workshop curriculum: "the desire to establish a world for children that is richer, larger, more colorful, and more accessible than the one we have known" (p. xii).

Writing workshop approaches have sought to enrich children's (and teachers') lives in schools by allowing them to bring their pulsing worlds into the mechanical, dry space. What these approaches have largely ignored is how to enrich children's worlds with critical work on texts— work that would enlarge, affirm, and call into question the experiences children bring with them from family and community. Teachers of writing should embrace the curricular task of identifying texts upon which (and against which) children and teachers will work. These texts would be at the center of at least some of the collective projects children pursue in classrooms. Other projects would focus on producing (reproducing) certain genres and forms—as in genre studies.

Where do we get these important texts, and how do we know one when we see one? Part of the answer to the second question rests with who gets to say a text is important or not. Adults and children are two groups with consequential assessments of the relative importance of various texts, and of course, these assessments can be at odds. One of the challenges of collective writing projects will be finding texts that both groups deem worthy of attention and labor (the difficulty of which Dewey (1956) underestimated, I think, in his *The Child and the Curriculum*). I do not underestimate the difficulty of this task, but will only note here that workshop approaches have traditionally solved this problem by giving responsibility over to children for selecting the important texts—that is, the personal narratives and descriptions drawn from children's memories and interests. Atwell (1987) writes that workshops are "student-centered in the sense that individuals' rigorous pursuit of their own ideas is the course content" (p. 41). But there are at least two other sources teachers and students might draw on for important texts. These sources are what I will call the official and unofficial canons (see Carroll, 1988, for his discussion of what I am calling the unofficial canon—his term is "vulgar canon").

Critical work with the official canon—with the texts that are already in schools and classrooms, that have already been certified as important for children by teachers, parents, university experts, state and federal policies—is essential. This canon is represented by children's books in the library, reading basals, and language arts, math, and history textbooks. There are, of course, continuing struggles over this canon on many levels within the educational system and across society—from parent efforts to censor novels for young adults in the library, to the adoption by teacher and administration committees of this and not that basal series, to Hirsch (1987) prescribing the story of George Washington and the Cherry Tree as a neutral bit of information we need to read (I side with McLaren, 1988, in his critical response to Hirsch and other exponents of "cultural literacy").

The unofficial canon is made up of texts children encounter in their homes and on the streets—movies, cartoons, TV shows, song lyrics, jokes, magazines, stories told them in catechisms and by their parents and grandparents. These texts are, as Carroll (1988) notes, often much more important to students than texts from the official canon. It might seem strange for teachers to appropriate some of these texts for use in workshops, especially if our goals are to enlarge and transform the everyday worlds of our children—these texts are part of the everyday. But the inclusion of texts from the unofficial canon is important for at least three reasons.

First, these texts are important to children. TV shows about Freddy Krueger and the Teenage Mutant Ninja Turtles, and Mom's story about accidently popping a wheelie on a motorcycle, are texts children choose to bring into the writing workshop themselves, exactly because these texts interest them and are important for their experiences. This does not mean that any particular text from the unofficial canon will be important to all children—several children in my class, for example, were much more interested in the chapter in their science textbook on the solar system than they were with the Ninja Turtles. Second, as unofficial texts, these texts often contain oppositional elements important for criticism of more official ones (Shor, 1986). That is, the clash of meanings and values that occur as unofficial and official canons are brought into interaction has promise for helping us and children understand both sets of texts better.

Finally, and perhaps most importantly, if our goal is to enlarge and transform the worlds of children, then one of the ways we can do this is by helping them learn to read and question the everyday texts of the unofficial canon. Scholes (1989) provides stunning examples of such reading and criticism in his analysis of a beer commercial that sells its beer as we root for the black baseball umpire in his showdown with a grizzled, white manager, "because we want the system to work—not just baseball but the whole thing: America" (p. 123); and in his analysis of magazine advertising that "goes for the sexual jugular" (p. 118). Christensen (1991) and Pang (1991) discuss such work with high school and elementary students, in projects that examine children's stories, cartoons, and films for their stereotypical race and gender portrayals.

My point is that we do not want the textual power of these pervasive texts from the unofficial canon to overpower our students. I should emphasize, however, that we want to take a similar stance to the texts of the official canon as well. They wield considerable textual power, particularly with the various institutional endorsements that make them official. We do not want children to give themselves over to these texts too quickly or too easily—to their "beauty and depths of information."

Collective writing projects with important texts as "problems to be solved"—either in the production of certain genres of texts, or in the reading, interpretation, and criticism of texts—hold promise for our goals of helping children empower themselves in their reading and writing. The expansion of the curriculum of writing workshops to include critical work with important texts from official and unofficial canons could enlarge children's repertoire of forms and purposes for writing, and enrich and transform their conceptions of themselves and the world around them. In addition to these possible benefits, I see at least three other reasons for considering collective writing projects.

The first is that such projects may reduce risks associated with writing and self-exposure for students. Writing workshop approaches have focused on personal narratives and topics. Collective projects, while allowing for and encouraging personal stances and individualized solutions to textual problems, would focus on texts and their production and criticism, rather than on children's personal lives. The risk of exposure, on some level, is unavoidable: When we write or speak we make assertions and express interests and values, and these can be discerned and criticized. But in collective projects, children's *texts* would be shared and exposed, not necessarily their personal lives. Children may feel more comfortable asserting themselves in the public spaces workshops provide, if the demand is not made that they put so much of themselves there (McCarthey, 1992). (Obviously, the study and writing of autobiographies, for example, would reintroduce risks related to exposure of personal material, as might biographies of parents, relatives.)

Second, there seem to be greater possibilities for community-building in workshops with collective projects than in workshops with individualized ones. I associate these possibilities with the focus for children's activity that collective problems provide. The focus on producing and/or criticizing specific texts may lessen chances for children to turn on each other. Children's activity can turn to many ends, some of which we want to support, others which we do not. With collective projects, we support certain peer relations, not by intervening at the level of outward behavior, but at the level of curriculum, by directing their attention to a common problem to be solved. Furthermore, collective problems at the center of activity may mean that individual contributions can "add up," contribute towards the knowledge of the group as it tries to solve textual problems, in ways that individual solutions to individual problems do not. There seems a better chance that children themselves will see and acknowledge the contributions of others when those contributions help in common efforts to produce or respond to important texts.

Finally, and related to possibilities for community-building, collective projects assume and project a vision of empowerment that I find more in line with my own notions of change as a product of individual and collective struggle. Workshop advocates, when they consider the relation of their work to larger societal and political issues, tend to conceive of change in terms of individual action and dissent. Berlin (1988) provides a powerful reading and critique of workshop approaches firmly embedded within what he calls an "expressionistic rhetoric." He argues that this rhetoric, represented most ably by writers such as Murray and Elbow, does provide a powerful "denunciation of economic, political, and social pressures to conform" (p. 486). The problem for Berlin is that while this rhetoric champions resistance to dehumanizing forces and conditions, it is always (and only) individual resistance:

> The only hope in a society working to destroy the uniqueness of the individual is for each of us to assert our individuality against the tyranny of the authoritarian corporation, state, and society. Strategies for doing so must of course be left to the individual, each lighting one small candle in order to create a brighter world. (p. 487)

Grant Berlin his sarcasm, and his point. Workshop approaches emphasize individual voice and projects, and, as I learned in this third grade classroom, these projects can pursue ends in conflict with our hopes for a classroom community in which children respect one another, and all children feel safe and supported in their efforts to acquire power over the texts they read and write. Collective classroom projects offer the possibility that children will learn how to work together, and learn the value of such collective efforts in solving problems that they face. I am not envisioning some always-friendly, smooth classroom of consensus. I am envisioning an engaged pluralistic community, in which differences among children promote learning (and are not necessarily resolved). Collective projects hold out the possibility that children will recognize the power of joining together and sharing their knowledge and strength; they hold out the possibility of undermining some of the individualism and competition our schools and society often engender.

———

Possibilities. I have suggested two re-visions for writing workshop approaches: a critically pragmatic teacher response to children's texts that is sensitive to the meanings and consequences of those texts for the immediate classroom community, and collective projects in which the production and criticism of important texts serves to focus children and teachers' work in the workshop. Both re-visions call for teacher intervention in the lives and work of children in writing workshops.

If I erred in my attempts to influence children's writing and peer relations in my teaching at Clifford, I erred on the side of trying *not* to overdetermine children's actions in the room. This entailed risks and consequences, which I have explored in previous chapters. But teacher efforts to take greater control of the shape and content of children's literacy work have their own dangers. If writing is messy, purposeful, "novel" (Doyle, 1986) work, then, with increased teacher control, we risk denying children the chance to find reasons to write that motivate and sustain them, and the space to maneuver and work out creative and divergent responses to textual problems.

A story told by Oliver Sacks (1990) about his early work with patients suffering from migraine will sharpen my point, and deserves extended quotation.

> My first thoughts were that migraine was a simple pathology . . . which would require a pill, a medication, and that the beginning and end of medicine was to make the diagnosis and to give the pill. But there were many patients who shook me. One in particular was a young mathematician who described to me how every week he had a sort of cycle. He would start to get nervous and irritable on Wednesday, and this would become worse by Thursday; by Friday, he could not work. On Saturday he was greatly agitated, and on Sunday he would have a terrible migraine. But then, toward afternoon, the migraine would die away. . . . As the migraine and the tension drained out of this man, he would feel himself refreshed, renewed, he would feel calm and creative, and on Sunday evening, Monday, and Tuesday, he did original work in mathematics. Then he would start getting irritable again.
>
> When I "cured" this man of his migraines, I also "cured" him of his mathematics. Along with the pathology, the creativity also dis-

appeared, and this made it clear that one had to inspect the economy of the person, the economy of this strange cycle of illness and
misery each week culminating in a migraine and then followed by
a wonderful transcendent sort of health and creativity. It is not suf-
ficient just to make a diagnosis of migraine and give a pill. (p. 45)

The pill we must avoid is reasserting a stifling, silencing teacher control over the talk and texts of children. The last thing I want is for my
work to provide excuses for such a move.

In order to respond to workshop advocates' Romantic portrayals of
children and writing in workshops, I have emphasized some of the problems that attended increased student control over the work of literacy. I
have examined the underside of peer relations in this classroom, and how
children's texts participated in those relations. One way to stop possibly
harmful elements of children's experiences and relations from influencing
the texts and processes of writing classrooms is to relegate children's lives
to the playground and to the edges of tightly controlled classroom activities. But this we must refuse to do. Tightening teacher control may discourage attempts by children to use their writing to hurt or belittle others.
It will also discourage the writing of *The Second Stories Club*, and *Sleeping
Beauty*, and *The Cloud That Smiled*. The "teacher control" pill, like the pill
Sacks gave his patient the mathematician, would cure children's active
engagement and exploration of writing as it cured other pathologies.

We should not give up on goals of helping students develop their
voices in ways artistic and political, even though it is difficult, risky work.
Thus far, workshop advocates have helped us most in understanding the
craft aspects of writing, and how we as teachers can support children
learning this craft. But a focus on craft, without serious consideration of
the intentions young writers pursue, and the material they appropriate
and transform, is irresponsible. It ignores the rhetorical consequences of
children's texts *for children* as audiences and members of a classroom
community. It denies children, as writers, the opportunity to engage in
conversations about the knowledge, beliefs, and values they draw upon
and express in their texts.

With the re-visions of critically pragmatic response and collective
writing projects, I tried to point to something better, point to more effective and responsible ways to intervene in the work of children in writing
workshops. My hope for these re-visions is that they generate searching,
lively discussions among children and teachers, about writing and its
responsibilities; that they make workshops more hospitable, supportive
places for all children to write themselves and their worlds on the page.

As I write this, my son, John Jacob, is 5 years old; my daughter,

Sarah, is 2. My experiences with them, and my experiences as a teacher with my third grade students in this writing workshop, have confirmed me in the belief that children need help from adults—they need help directing their lives, in and out of school. But I also know that schools have traditionally over-directed children's lives and work. Writing workshop and Freirean critiques of schooling have responded exactly to the reduction of meaningful, complex work with texts, to dry, routinized tasks that deaden and routinize children themselves.

What I have struggled to express here is what my students and I struggled for in the writing workshop: some sort of balance. We must recognize that children need room to talk and act in order to learn and develop. We must also recognize that children's talk and actions can be turned to worthy and less worthy ends, and that as teachers we have the responsibility to push for worthy ones.

Worthy ones, for me, are those that envision classroom and future communities for children in which all members participate in the creation and recreation of the forms of life that constrain and sustain them. Communities in which Karen, Rajesh, William, Jil, Robert, Janis, and John boldly name themselves heros of their own stories. Communities in which Jessie fights off the evil spell cast by peers and is line leader once in a while.

Appendix

Additional Notes on the Study

I was concerned that the following discussions—of the use of pseudonyms, the length of the study, and beginning research questions—would disrupt the continuity of the early chapters. I have included them in this appendix as a supplement to those chapters.

THE USE OF PSEUDONYMS

Pseudonyms have been used for all students, staff, and parents who appear in my text. Pseudonyms have also been used *within* children's texts and other classroom documents. With reproductions of children's texts in figures, the procedure was to either white-out the actual names of the participants or to cover them with a small piece of paper and then hand write or type pseudonyms in the blank spaces created. Photocopies of these "original" documents were then made.

Many children used the names of classmates and themselves in their texts. I argue in chapters 3–6 that the meanings of children's texts were often heavily dependent on this use of children's names. I "doctored" original documents in this way, then, in order to aid readers' understanding of children's texts and my interpretations of them.

At times, I had to be creative in my use of pseudonyms in my text and in quotations from my fieldnotes. For example, in chapter 6, the unconventional spelling of one of the children's names was important for my interpretation of another child's story. Thus, I used an unusual spelling of the name Jill ("Jil"), as a pseudonym throughout my text. I also altered fieldnotes that I quote in that chapter to fit the pseudonym—instead of the original discussion of how the child's actual name was unconventional, I noted how "Jil" was spelled with only one "l" and how this might provide a clue to the interpretation of another child's story.

LENGTH OF THE STUDY

At several points in chapters 1 and 2, I comment that I taught writing 5 days a week throughout the 1989–90 school year. I want to provide a bit more specification of the length of the study, however, since I do not report on the entire year's teaching in this text.

My study focuses on the students' and my experiences of the writing workshop. Our writing workshop ran from the beginning of the school year (late August) through the end of March. There was one extended break from the writing workshop during these months. Children left for the winter holidays on December 20 and didn't return until the 2nd week of January. However, even then, the workshop did not begin again until the 1st week of February, for several reasons. I wanted to concentrate for a few weeks on an undergraduate course for future teachers that I was teaching at the university, and I had some writing I wanted to finish. In addition, Grace had several weeks' worth of standardized tests to administer in January and she had been concerned about finding time for them. Consequently, when I suggested in December that I might not begin the workshop immediately after the holidays, Grace readily agreed. She used writing workshop time for these tests. She also used the break from writing workshop to catch up in other subject areas.

Thus, the writing workshop ran for approximately 5½ months of the school year, and my text is based primarily in the teaching and data collection I pursued during those months.

The workshop was officially "shut down" just before the children's spring break. Our work together after the break was organized differently than it had been in the writing workshop. In fact, during April and May my students and I pursued what I call a "collective writing project" in chapter 7. Children wrote biographies of important women in their lives (including mothers, grandmothers, aunts, teachers), after a series of experiences including reading published biographies and interviewing women from the community. Individual biographies were collected and published in a volume entitled *Important Women in Our Lives*. Each child received a copy, and a copy was also given to the Clifford library—the librarian attended our presentation of the volume to the school principal and attached an official call number and check-out card to it as part of the ceremony. Around the edges of these activities, colleagues and I prepared for and conducted extended interviews of children. These interviews focused on children's experiences of the writing workshop.

BEGINNING RESEARCH QUESTIONS

In an early memo characterizing my study, I wrote that "two broad areas for investigation and analysis . . . linked to the writing workshop approach's conception of the teacher role" would guide at least my initial research in the field (Memo, 7-27-89). I noted that the emphases were tentative, since one of the purposes of the project was to identify the special problems and issues that attended teaching and learning within writing workshop classrooms. I characterized the first broad area of concern as follows:

> A key task for writing workshop teachers is establishing a classroom environment that supports growth in writing. What is involved in setting up such an environment? Graves and Calkins, of course, offer practical suggestions, but what actually happens when a teacher attempts to teach in this way? What enables and constrains teacher efforts to establish such an environment? What materials, routines, and classroom norms are involved? What (if any) changes in materials, routines, and norms occur across a school year? (Memo, 7-27-89)

This first group of questions was informed by ethnographic and sociolinguistic reports of classrooms in which teachers and students misunderstood each other because they were acting on different assumptions of what was appropriate behavior and speech (e.g., Heath, 1983; Philips, 1983; Michaels, 1981). Misunderstanding was likely as my students and I groped to figure out how to do things in a classroom with new materials, routines and norms. The last two questions, especially, show an ethnographic interest in describing what patterns of interaction actually emerged, and possible changes in those patterns as the year progressed.

But there was also a fairly strong teacher-researcher flavor to these questions. As Cochran-Smith and Lytle (1990) note:

> The unique feature of questions that prompt teacher research is that they emanate solely neither from theory nor from practice, but from the critical reflection on the intersection of the two. (p. 6)

I was interested in what actually happened when I tried to enact a certain vision of teaching and learning writing in the classroom; I was interested in the "discrepancies between what is intended and what occurs"

(Cochran-Smith and Lytle, 1990, p. 5). In a later proposal, I appropriated Berthoff's (1987) notion of the classroom as a philosophical laboratory, and said that the strength of my work rested on bringing "theory to bear on practice even as practice corrects theory" (Proposal, 11-89).

The second broad area of concern looked to the writing conference:

> The primary instructional strategy within the writing workshop approach is the writing conference, a teacher-student conversation about student texts and writing processes. What happens within these writing conferences? From the teacher's perspective, what difficulties are involved with responding to young writers' written texts? From the students' perspective, how do writing conferences help or hinder their writing? How do these conferences influence the writing that children do in the classroom? (Memo, 7-27-89)

These questions, especially the first three, were informed by a small body of research on teacher-student writing conferences that suggests that breaking out of traditional teacher-dominated patterns, and embracing the models put forward by Murray (1985), Graves (1983), and Calkins (1986)—what I call following the child in chapter 1—may actually be quite difficult. Jacob (1982), for example, in a study of writing conferences in a junior college setting, found that teachers controlled writing conferences much as they did traditional lessons; Jacob described the discourse as "unilateral, from instructor to student" (p. 386). Michaels, Ulichney, and Watson-Gegeo (1986), and Freedman (1987), found that teacher goals and implicit expectations for children's writing tasks overpowered student intentions in the writing conferences of sixth and ninth grade students.

Florio-Ruane (1991) suggests various sources of difficulties in transforming writing conference talk: contextual constraints such as limited time, mandated curriculum, and the school's evaluative climate; the knowledge (often limited) that teachers and students bring of writing processes, schooling, and each other, to their conversations; and traditional discourse patterns that make it difficult for students to "assume rights to initiate talk, determine topic, or serve as 'experts' even about their own writing problems and purposes" (p. 374). Ulichney and Watson-Gegeo (1989) point to mandated writing tests, minimal support for teacher efforts to transform practice, and pressure to improve achievement test scores as factors that undermine workshop and process writing efforts and goals.

I was interested in what would happen when I tried to enact a different sort of school talk in writing conferences. I was particularly interested in the difficulties attending response as socioanalysis (discussed in chapter 1). Why? Simply supporting student intentions and material in writing conferences—following the child—appeared to be hard enough to accomplish. Response as socioanalysis required me to support *and* question student material. In *questioning* that material, from my position of authority in the classroom, I once again ran the *risk* of shutting down, silencing student voice in the classroom. Rather than pushing our thought and action forward to a more critical evaluation of our situation, response as socioanalysis could encourage students to not speak their mind, or to look for the correct thing to say to please the teacher.

The final question above, about the influence writing conferences had on student writing, was motivated by my growing theoretical interest in Bakhtin. I was interested in examining how children appropriated what was said in the writing conferences for their future efforts at writing and revision. How would children (if they did) appropriate teacher words for their own purposes in their texts? Would they appropriate the teacher's words, or would the teacher's words appropriate them? The teacher-student writing conference seemed a particularly interesting place to "test" Bakhtin's work, and see what purchase it provided on a complex speaking/writing situation involving participants who brought varying purposes and unequal power to their talk.

References

Applebee, A. N. (1981). *Writing in the secondary school: English and the content areas.* Urbana, IL: National Council of Teachers of English.

Applebee, A. N. (1986). Problems in process approaches: Toward a reconceptualization of process instruction. In A. Petrosky & D. Bartholomae (Eds.), *The teaching of writing* (pp. 95–113). Chicago: University of Chicago.

Atwell, N. (1987). *In the middle: Writing, reading, and learning with adolescents.* Portsmouth, NH: Boynton/Cook.

Bakhtin, M. M. (1981). *The dialogic imagination.* Austin: University of Texas.

Bakhtin, M. M. (1986). *Speech genres and other late essays.* Austin: University of Texas.

Barnes, D., & Barnes, D. (1984). *Versions of English.* London: Heinemann.

Barthes, R. (1974). *S/Z.* New York: Farrar, Strauss and Giroux.

Benhabib, S. (1992). *Situating the self: Gender, community and postmodernism in contemporary ethics.* New York: Routledge.

Bereiter, C., & Scardamalia, M. (1982). From conversation to composition: The role of instruction in a developmental process. In R. Glaser (Ed.), *Advances in instructional psychology* (Vol. 2, pp. 1–64). Hillsdale, NJ: Erlbaum.

Berlin, J. (1988). Rhetoric and ideology in the writing class. *College English, 50*(5), 477–494.

Bernstein, R. J. (1988). Pragmatism, pluralism, and the healing of wounds. *American Philosophical Association Proceedings, 63*(3), 5–18.

Berthoff, A. (1987). From dialogue to dialectic to dialogue. In D. Goswami & P. R. Stillman (Eds.), *Reclaiming the classroom: Teacher research as an agency for change* (pp. 75–86). Portsmouth, NH: Heinemann.

Besley, C. (1986). The romantic construction of the unconscious. In F. Barker, P. Hulme, M. Iverson, & D. Loxley (Eds.), *Literature, politics and theory* (pp. 57–76). London: Methuen.

Bissex, G., & Bullock, R. (1987). *Seeing for ourselves: Case study research by teachers of writing.* Portsmouth, NH: Heinemann.

Bogdan, R. C., & Biklen, S. K. (1982). *Qualitative research for education: An introduction to theory and methods.* Boston: Allyn and Bacon.

Britton, J. (1978). The composing processes and the functions of writing. In C. R. Cooper & L. Odell (Eds.), *Research on composing: Points of departure* (pp. 13–28). Urbana, IL: National Council of Teachers of English.

Britton, J. (1982). Spectator role and the beginning of writing. In M. Nystrand (Ed.), *What writers know: The language, process and structure of written discourse* (pp. 149–169). New York: Academic.

Brooke, R. (1987). Lacan, transference, and writing instruction. *College English,* 49(6), 679–691.

Bruner, J. (1990). *Acts of meaning.* Cambridge, MA: Harvard University.

Burton, F. R. (1985). *The reading-writing connection: A one year teacher-as-researcher study of third-fourth grade writers and their literary experiences.* Unpublished doctoral dissertation, Ohio State University.

Calkins, L. M. (1983). *Lessons from a child: On the teaching and learning of writing.* Portsmouth, NH: Heinemann.

Calkins, L. M. (1986). *The art of teaching writing.* Portsmouth, NH: Heinemann.

Calkins, L. M. (1991). *Living between the lines.* Portsmouth, NH: Heinemann.

Carroll, J. (1988). *The vulgar canon and its uses in the classroom.* Paper presented at annual meeting of the Conference on College Composition and Communication, St. Louis, MO.

Cazden, C. B. (1986). Classroom discourse. In M. C. Wittrock (Ed.), *Handbook of research on teaching* (3rd ed., pp. 432–463). New York: MacMillan.

Cherryholmes, C. (1988). *Power and criticism: Poststructural investigations in education.* New York: Teachers College.

Cherryholmes, C. (1990). *Reading research.* Unpublished manuscript.

Christensen, L. (1991). Unlearning the myths that bind us. *Rethinking Schools,* 5(4), 1–17.

Cochran-Smith, M., & Lytle, S. L. (1990). Research on teaching and teacher research: The issues that divide. *Educational Researcher, 19*(2), 2–11.

Connell, R. W., Dowsett, G. W., Kessler, S., & Aschenden, D. J. (1982). *Making the difference.* Boston: Allen and Unwin.

Delpit, L. D. (1988). The silenced dialogue: Power and pedagogy in educating other people's children. *Harvard Educational Review, 58*(3), 280–298.

deMan, P. (1979). *Allegories of reading: Figural language in Rousseau, Nietzsche, Rilke, and Proust.* New Haven: Yale University.

Dewey, J. (1956). *The child and the curriculum* and *The school and society.* Chicago: University of Chicago.

Doyle, W. (1986). Content representation in teachers' definitions of academic work. *Journal of Curriculum Studies, 18*(4), 365–379.

Dyson, A. H. (1989). *Multiple worlds of child writers: Friends learning to write.* New York: Teachers College.

Eagleton, T. (1983). *Literary theory: An introduction.* Minneapolis: University of Minnesota.

Eagleton, T. (1991). *Ideology: An introduction.* London: Verso.

Elbow, P. (1973). *Writing without teachers.* London: Oxford University.

Elbow, P. (1987). Closing my eyes as I speak: An argument for ignoring audience. *College English, 49*(1), 50–69.

Erickson, F. (1986). Qualitative methods in research on teaching. In M. C. Wittrock (Ed.), *Handbook on research on teaching* (3rd ed., pp. 119–161). New York: MacMillan.

Erickson, F., & Shultz, J. (1992). Student's experience of the curriculum. In P. Jackson (Ed.), *Handbook of research on curriculum* (pp. 465–485). New York: Macmillan.

Everhart, R. B. (1983). *Reading, writing and resistance: Adolescence and labor in a junior high school.* Boston: Routledge & Kegan Paul.

Faigley, L. (1986). Competing theories of process: A critique and a proposal. *College English, 48*(6), 527–542.

Flax, J. (1990). *Thinking fragments: Psychoanalysis, feminism and postmodernism in the contemporary West.* Berkeley, CA: University of California.

Florio-Ruane, S. (1991). Instructional conversations in learning to write and learning to teach. In L. Idol & B. Jones (Eds.), *Educational values and cognitive instruction: Implications for reform* (pp. 365–386). New York: Erlbaum.

Florio-Ruane, S., & Dunn, S. (1985). *Teaching writing: Some perennial questions and some possible answers* (Occasional Paper No. 85). East Lansing, MI: Institute for Research on Teaching, Michigan State University.

Florio-Ruane, S., & Lensmire, T. (1989). The role of instruction in learning to write. In J. Brophy (Ed.), *Advances in research on teaching* (pp. 73–103). Greenwich, CT: JAI.

Freedman, S. W. (1987). *Peer response in two ninth-grade classrooms* (Technical Report No. 12). Berkeley, CA: University of California, Center for the Study of Writing.

Freire, P. (1970). *Pedagogy of the oppressed.* New York: Continuum.

Freire, P. (1985). *The politics of education: Culture, power and liberation.* South Hadley, MA: Bergin and Garvey.

Freire, P., & Macedo, D. (1987). *Literacy: Reading the word and the world.* South Hadley, MA: Bergin and Garvey.

Gay, P. (1988). Freud: *A life for our time.* New York: W. W. Norton.

Gilbert, R. (1989). Student text as pedagogical text. In S. deCastell, A. Luke, & C. Luke (Eds.), *Language, authority and criticism: Readings on the school textbook* (pp. 195–202) London: Falmer.

Gilligan, C. (1982). *In a different voice: Psychological theory and women's development.* Cambridge, MA: Harvard University.

Giroux, H. (1988). Literacy and the pedagogy of voice and political empowerment. *Educational Theory, 38*(1), 61–75.

Giroux, H., & Simon, R. (1989). Popular culture and critical pedagogy: Everyday life as a basis for curriculum knowledge. In H. Giroux & P. McLaren (Eds.), *Critical pedagogy, the state, and cultural struggle* (pp. 236–252). New York: SUNY.

Glaser, B., & Strauss, A. L. (1967). *The discovery of grounded theory: Strategies for qualitative research.* Chicago: Aldine.

Goodman, J. (1992). *Elementary schooling for democracy.* Albany, NY: SUNY.

Goswami, D., & Stillman, P. (1987). *Reclaiming the classroom: Teacher research as an agency for change.* Upper Montclair, NJ: Boynton/Cook.

Graves, D. (1981). Renters and owners: Donald Graves on writing. *English Magazine, 8,* 4–7.

Graves, D. (1983). *Writing: Teachers and children at work.* Portsmouth, NH: Heinemann.

Graves, D., & Hansen, J. (1983). The author's chair. *Language Arts, 60*(2), 176–83.

Grumet, M. R. (1988). *Bitter milk: Women and teaching.* Amherst: University of Massachusetts.

Habermas, J. (1970). Toward a theory of communicative competence. In H. P. Dreitzel (Ed.), *Recent sociology no. 2: Patterns of communicative behavior* (pp. 115–148). New York: Macmillan.

Habermas, J. (1984). *The theory of communicative action: Reason and the rationality of society* (vol. 1). (T. McCarthy, Trans.). Boston: Beacon.

Habermas, J. (1987). *The theory of communicative action: Lifeworld and system: A critique of functionalist reason* (vol. 2). (T. McCarthy, Trans.). Boston: Beacon.

Hairston, M. (1982). The winds of change: Thomas Kuhn and the revolution in the teaching of writing. *College Composition and Communication, 33*(1), 76–88.

Hammersly, M., & Atkinson, P. (1983). *Ethnography: Principles in practice*. London: Tavistock.

Harris, J. (1987). The plural text/the plural self: Roland Barthes and William Coles. *College English, 49*(2), 158–170.

Harris, J. (1989). The idea of community in the study of writing. *College Composition and Communication, 40*(1), 11–22.

Heath, S. B. (1983). *Ways with words: Language, life, and work in communities and classrooms*. Cambridge: Cambridge University.

Hirsch, E. D. (1987). *Cultural literacy: What every American needs to know*. Boston: Houghton Mifflin.

Hogan, D. (1989). *Capitalism and conscience in the classroom: Social structure and pedagogy in ante-bellum New England*. Unpublished manuscript.

Hogan, K. (1987). Breaking patterns. In G. L. Bissex & R. H. Bullock (Eds), *Seeing for ourselves: Case study research by teachers of writing* (pp. 173–181). Portsmouth, NH: Heinemann.

Hooks, B. (1989). *Talking back: Thinking feminist—thinking black*. Boston: South Hadley.

Hulbert, M. (1987). *Ideology, process and subjectivity: The role of hermeneutics in the writing conference*. Paper presented at the annual meeting of the Conference on College Composition and Communication, Atlanta, GA.

Jacob, G. P. (1982). An ethnographic study of the writing conference: The degree of student involvement in the writing process. *Dissertation Abstracts International, 43,* 386A. (University Microfilms No. 8216050).

Koch, K. (1973). *Rose, where did you get that red?* New York: Vintage Books.

Kristeva, J. (1986). *The Kristeva reader* (T. Moi, Ed.). New York: Columbia University.

LaCapra, D. (1983). *Rethinking intellectual history: texts, contexts, language*. Ithaca, NY: Cornell University.

London, P. (1986). *The modes and morals of psychotherapy* (2nd ed.). Washington, DC: Hemisphere.

Martin, J. R. (1989). *Factual writing: Exploring and challenging social reality*. Oxford: Oxford University.

McCarthey, S. (1992). *Risks and opportunities of writing from personal experience*. Paper presented at the National Reading Conference, San Antonio, Texas.

McGee, P. (1987). *Truth and resistance: Teaching as a form of analysis*. College English, 49(6), 667–678.

McLaren, P. (1988). Culture or canon? Critical pedagogy and the politics of literacy. *Harvard Educational Review, 58*(2), 213–234.

McLeod, A. (1986). Critical literacy: Taking control of our own lives. *Language Arts, 63*(1), 37–50.

Mehan, H. (1979). *Learning lessons.* Cambridge, MA: Harvard University.

Mehan, H. (1982). The structure of classroom events and their consequences for student performance. In P. Gilmore and A. Glatthorn (Eds.), *Children in and out of school: Ethnography and education* (pp. 59–87). Washington, DC: Center for Applied Linguistics.

Michaels, S. (1981). "Sharing time": Children's narrative styles and differential access to literacy. *Language in Society, 10,* 423–442.

Michaels, S., Ulichney, P., & Watson-Gageo, K. (1986). *Social processes and written products: Teacher expectations, writing conferences, and student texts.* Paper presented at the annual meeting of the American Educational Research Association, San Francisco.

Miller, J. H. (1990). Narrative. In F. Lentricchia & T. McLaughlin (Eds.), *Critical terms for literary study* (pp. 66–79). Chicago: University of Chicago.

Murphy, A. (1989). Transference and resistance in the basic writing classroom: Problematics and praxis. *College Composition and Communication, 40*(2), 175–187.

Murray, D. (1968). *A writer teaches writing: A practical method of teaching composition.* Boston: Houghton Mifflin.

Murray, D. (1979). The listening eye: Reflections on the writing conference. *College English, 41*(1), 13–18.

Murray, D. (1985). *A writer teaches writing.* Boston: Houghton Mifflin.

Paley, V. (1989). *White teacher.* Cambridge, MA: Harvard University.

Paley, V. (1990). *The boy who would be a helicopter.* Cambridge, MA: Harvard University.

Pang, V. O. (1991). Teaching children about social issues: Kidpower. In C. Sleeter (Ed.), *Empowerment through multicultural education* (pp. 179–197). Albany, NY: SUNY.

Pechey, G. (1986). Bakhtin, Marxism and post-structuralism. In F. Barker, P. Hulme, M. Iverson, & D. Loxley (Eds.), *Literature, politics and theory* (pp. 104–125). London: Methuen.

Philips, S. (1983). *The invisible culture: Communication in the classroom and community on the Warm Springs Indian Reservation.* New York: Longman.

Rorty, R. (1989). *Contingency, irony, and solidarity.* Cambridge, MA: Harvard University.

Richards, P. (1986). Risk. In H. Becker, (Ed.) *Writing for social scientists: How to start and finish your thesis, book or article* (pp. 109–120). Chicago: University of Chicago.

Sacks, O. (1990). Neurology and the soul. *The New York Review of Books, 37*(18), 44–50.

Said, E. (1983). *The world, the text, and the critic.* Cambridge, MA: Harvard University.

Scholes, R. E. (1985). *Textual power: Literary theory and the teaching of English.* New Haven: Yale University.

Scholes, R. E. (1989). *Protocols of Reading*. New Haven: Yale University.

Schwartz, L. S. (1990). True confessions of a reader. *Salamagundi, 88,* 176–228.

Scollon, R. (1988). Storytelling, reading, and the micropolitics of literacy. In R.S. Baldwin (Ed.), *Dialogues in literacy research* (pp. 115–133). Chicago: National Reading Conference.

Shor, I. (1986). *Cultural wars: School and society in the conservative restoration, 1969–1984.* Boston: Routledge & Kegan Paul.

Simon, H. A. (1957). *Models of man*. New York: John Wiley.

Sollors, W. (1990). Ethnicity. In F. Lentricchia & T. McLaughlin (Eds.), *Critical terms for literary study*. Chicago: University of Chicago.

Temple, C., Nathan, R., Burris, N., & Temple, F. (1988). *The beginnings of writing* (2nd ed.). Boston: Allyn and Bacon.

Thoreau, H. (1960). *Walden*. New York: New American Library.

Thorne, B. (1986). Girls and boys together . . . but mostly apart: Gender arrangements in elementary schools. In W. Hargup & Z. Rubin (Eds.), *Relationships and development* (pp. 167–184). Hillsdale, NJ: Lawrence Erlbaum Associates.

Ulichney, P., & Watson-Gageo, K. (1989). Interactions and authority: The dominant interpretative framework in writing conferences. *Discourse Processes, 12,* 309–328.

Volosinov, V. (1973). *Marxism and the philosophy of language.* (L. Matejka & I. R. Titumink, Trans.). Cambridge, MA: Harvard University.

Volosinov, V. (1976). *Freudianism: A Marxist critique.* (I.R. Titunik, Trans.). New York: Academic.

Vygotsky, L. S. (1978). *Mind in society: The development of higher psychological processes*. Cambridge, MA: Harvard University.

Vygotsky, L. S. (1979). The prehistory of written language. In M. Martlew (Ed.), *The psychology of written language* (pp. 105–119). Chichester: John Wiley and Sons.

Vygotsky, L. S. (1981). The genesis of higher mental functions. In J. Wertsch (Ed.), *The concept of activity in Soviet psychology* (pp. 144–187). Armonk, NY: M. E. Sharpe.

Waller, W. (1932). *The sociology of teaching*. New York: Wiley.

Wertsch, J. V. (1979). From social interaction to higher psychological processes: A clarification and application of Vygotsky's theory. *Human Development, 22,* 1–22.

Wertsch, J. V. (1985). Vygotsky: *The social formation of mind*. Cambridge, MA: Harvard University.

West, C. (1989). *The American evasion of philosophy: A genealogy of pragmatism.* Madison, WI: University of Wisconsin.

Widdowson, H. G. (1975). *Stylistics and the teaching of literature*. London: Longman.

Williams, R. (1983). *Culture and society: 1780–1950*. New York: Columbia University.

Willinsky, J. (1986). *The romance of expression as art versus education*. Paper presented as part of Concordia University Faculty of Fine Arts Graduate Studio Lecture Series.

Willinsky, J. (1990). *The new literacy: Redefining reading and writing in the schools*. New York: Routledge.

Willis, P. (1977). *Learning to labor*. Lexington, MA: Heath.

Young, R. (1990). *A critical theory of education: Habermas and our children's future*. New York: Teachers College.

Index

About the Author

TIMOTHY J. LENSMIRE is Assistant Professor of Education at Washington University in St. Louis, where he teaches courses on literacy and educational philosophy. He received his Ph.D. from Michigan State University, and has worked in elementary and junior high schools in Wisconsin, Michigan, and Missouri. His research interests include children's writing and literary and critical theory, especially the work of Mikhail Bakhtin.